Capitalism
and
Christianity

Capitalism

⊰ and ⊱

Christianity

*The Possibility of
Christian Personalism*

Richard C. Bayer

GEORGETOWN UNIVERSITY PRESS/WASHINGTON, D.C.

Georgetown University Press, Washington, D.C. 20007
©1999 by Georgetown University Press. All rights reserved.
Printed in the United States of America
10 9 8 7 6 5 4 3 2 1 1999
THIS VOLUME IS PRINTED ON ACID-FREE OFFSET BOOKPAPER.

Library of Congress Cataloging-in-Publication Data

Bayer, Richard C.
   Capitalism and Christianity : the possibility of Christian
personalism / Richard C. Bayer.
     p. cm.
   ISBN 0-87840-730-8 (cloth). — ISBN 0-87840-731-6 (paper)
   1. Capitalism—Religious aspects—Catholic Church.
2. Personalism—Economic aspects. I. Title.
BX1795.C35B38 1999
   261.8′5—dc21
                                                    99-18210
                                                       CIP

To Kate, Sara, Paul, and Martin

Contents

List of Tables

Acknowledgment

I want to acknowledge my debt of thanks to those scholars who have so courageously laid the groundwork in theology to make the development of a Personalist line of thought possible. I also owe a great debt of thanks to those teachers in my past whose influence guides many aspects of my thinking. There is an ancient proverb that says it is no credit to the master (teacher) if a student sits forever at his/her feet. That is surely the case here, as aspects of my method and content may be somewhat controversial. Lastly, I am much indebted to John Samples of Georgetown University Press for his insightful criticisms which helped to put the manuscript into acceptable form. All shortcomings remain, of course, my own responsibility.

Introduction

The collapse of socialism, and the almost worldwide appeal of market-oriented political economies, has made this among the most exciting of times for those in the field of Christian social ethics. European scholars for example are grappling with the emerging market economies of the former Eastern bloc countries, as well as with the expansion of free trade and other economic consequences of European unity. I recently returned from the 1997 meeting of the European *Societas Ethica* held in Gdansk-Oliwa and at which I presented a paper. The conference theme was "Solidarität & Sozialstaat" (Solidarity and Welfare State). As one would anticipate, the organization of the presentations at the conference demonstrated good ethical method: the first paper offered a description of the empirical problem and situation; subsequent papers reviewed historical and more recent theological and ecclesiastical documents dealing with such social ethical problems; followed finally by systematic discussion of how to bring theological and philosophical resources to bear on the current situation. What I did not fully anticipate was the remarkably negative view taken by these prominent and very scholarly figures in the profession toward the collapse of socialism and the rise of the market. The opening speaker from the Amsterdam School of Social Science Research began the conference in this way:

> At the moment a widespread feeling exists, all over Europe, of a growing domination of mere market forces at the expense of the social dimension. . . . We cannot yet speak of American-like ghetto's in Europe, but the structural economic conditions for the formation of ghettos exist in Europe nowadays and they will develop quite rapidly, if the economic revitalization is carried out without due

respect to the social integration of all the unemployed, young and old.

During the conference, it seemed customary, in fact almost obligatory, for speakers from the West to hurl anathemas at market political economies and their moral underpinnings. On the other hand, one witnessed much less of this when speakers from Poland, Estonia, and other countries formerly under Soviet rule spoke.

The practical call was for greater state intervention in the various spheres of economic and social life for the purpose of reducing income inequality, joblessness, poverty, and social anomie. Positively, from my perspective, there was recognition of the failures of the present (redistributive) "welfare state" and consideration of what Neil Gilbert calls the "enabling state." Unfortunately, my reading of the proposals and theoretical ideas under discussion was that even though they repeatedly referred to the "social dimension" of human existence almost like a mantra, the basic entities under examination remained the individual and the state. This is still a very individualistic analysis since, again from my view, the road to economic justice will begin with an extended consideration of the principle of the subsidiarity. Therefore the debate seems almost hopelessly ensnared in the rhetoric of libertarian freedom vs. state intervention in pursuit of the goal of meeting human economic needs.

Perhaps the most significant contribution of this book is the unique integration of moral argument with economic analysis. The book challenges the "orthodoxy" which emphasizes the role of central authorities in the achievement of economic justice by offering an alternative vision, drawing especially on the resources of Catholic Social Thought and orthodox economics. I will not argue that this vision is the only vision which can claim support from Catholic Social Thought; I do argue that it is strongly indicated, based on the research presented in chapter 1. Furthermore, while the book does presume work done from a neoconservative perspective and especially the work of the seminal thinker Michael Novak, differences in method and content from Novak's form of neoconservatism include the integration of moral analysis with economic data and theory; a greater recognition of the importance of reform in the economic sector; and especially the divergences in moral theory developed in chapter 4.

Recent years have seen a host of questions raised about what the proper role of the state should be in the lives of its citizens from the moral perspective. The practical bases for this concern in the United States are surveyed in chapter 2 from the time of the New Deal through the more contemporary emphasis on the enabling state. It has increasingly been recognized by policymakers that state intervention has generated serious disturbances in personal rights, initiative, and creativity. Precisely because the maintenance of full human agency became a problem under statist solutions to social problems in which "distributive justice" was the primary battle cry, recent reforms in the welfare state have come to stress decentralization and decategorization which yield a greater sphere of action and responsibility to more local levels. Of course, what these reforms often still do not recognize is the need to empower individuals who live *only in social communities* with others. In any case, the proper balance or antidote to this statism is not further emphasis on the isolated individual, but will have its source in an expanded understanding of the human person which accounts for human agency in the context of our varied social communities.

A major reality, and certainly the dominant problem from the moral perspective of the American system, is the persistence of terrible need in a "prosperous" land and the lack of full personal development of all persons and the whole person. The shortcomings of the applied ethical theory and technical efforts to reduce these inequities have challenged us to come to a better understanding of the human person and human agency. In chapter 3, I examine the social anthropology of contemporary liberal thought and practice that focuses on freedom, equality, and rationality, and I expand this social anthropology in chapter 4 along Personalist lines that draw especially from Catholic Social Thought.

A (Personalist) vision can be systematically advanced using the powers of the state to enable civil society and to *guide* movement toward (not implement) a more humane vision for economic life. We expect that any attempts to assist individuals that do not lead the able to work and to the fulfillment of a vocation will be inadequate from a moral (and not just an economic) perspective. The central task of an economic system is always to meet human needs and at the same time to provide for the development of human beings who exist in a context of social relations and support systems. From the moral and practical perspectives, these two cannot be separated, and they are achieved *simultaneously or not at all.*

Lest the vision in these chapters be accused of excessive abstractness or ambiguity about just how justice can be advanced when it is not literally implemented by the state, in chapter 5 I give a real-world example of a proposal that I believe would represent progress toward this vision. The "share economy" appears to receive a passing grade as a concrete example of a Personalist economic reform agenda. This Personalism is informed by philosophical liberalism and by theological sources, so it can and does take the market system and liberal economics as acceptable starting points by which to build a more just economy. It shows an appreciation of the social nature of the human person and advances solidarity among workers as they share a common fate. It promises to help meet human bodily and material needs since it promises greater microeconomic and macroeconomic efficiency. As creative and free human subjects, workers experience greater participation in profit sharing and decision making; alienation is thereby reduced. The share economy successfully moves past the older Keynesian agenda. Furthermore, the importance of decentralization, local responsibility and control, and especially nonstatist solutions to economic ills are morally relevant lessons incorporated into the reform. The reform also recognizes that the moral, cultural, and economic sectors are mutually conditioning and that also the economic sector must contribute to a political economy conceived along Personalist lines.

╼ I ╾

DEFENDING CAPITALISM
AGAINST ITS DESPISERS

1

Democratic Capitalism and Catholic Social Thought: A Moral Reassessment

Socialism is the only possible economic system from the Christian point of view. — Paul Tillich, 1957

In this chapter I examine certain developments in interpretation and also in theology that have taken place in Catholic Social Thought, and I indicate the empirical support for these developments. I will show how Catholic Social Thought has, correctly in my judgment, come to understand the senses in which market economies can serve as a basis to meet human needs and how market economies serve human persons best when the activity by the state is carefully and prudentially limited.

Perhaps the most appealing aspect of socialism (at least in theory) is the ability of social engineers to set the parameters for the distribution of society's benefits and burdens in such a way that all persons might have at least their basic needs meet. Injustice is eliminated through a redistribution of benefits and burdens primarily through the workings of the central political authority. In those societies which are irredeemably market oriented, this same sensibility has expressed itself in support of the welfare state. For Richard John Neuhaus, mainline religion in the United States is the "channel of continuity, the mainline of religious experience since the seventeenth century,"[1] and it includes the Presbyterian, Methodist, Episcopalian, and Congregationalist Churches. Roman Catholics and Lutherans are also in some ways mainline. Neuhaus is surely correct when he notes that since what economists have called "the Great

3

Contraction," or the depression of the 1930s in more popular terms, the mainline has aligned itself in its social mission with the left wing of the Democratic Party. The prayer is now "for the second coming of a George McGovern, assuming that FDR is no longer available."[2]

There is today a remarkable consensus or alignment among social ethicists in matters of political economy which has such hegemony that it may well undermine the creativity and relevance of Christian social ethics in addressing contemporary social problems. This book challenges the "orthodoxy" which emphasizes the role of central authorities in the achievement of economic justice by offering an alternative vision, drawing especially on the resources of Catholic Social Thought. I believe that three presuppositions define this basic orthodoxy and cry out for substantive analysis:

1. Market systems are a poor basis on which to meet human needs.
2. The essential economic problem in a market system is the exploitation of labor by capital.
3. Justice requires the state to expand its role in economic life.

In this first chapter I will show the developments in Catholic Social Thought on precisely these three points, and I will indicate the empirical support within orthodox macroeconomics for this development. At the very least, this will help to make a more positive moral assessment of the performance of the market system more comprehensible. So in this first chapter it is necessary for me to present information quite favorable to the market. Subsequent chapters will make clear the very large moral agenda that remains for market economies, especially in the United States.

The Present State of the Debate in Christian Ethics

In this past century, the attempt has been made to harness the extraordinary productivity of market economies to meet the needs of all persons, especially the poor. The term "welfare state" refers to a large constellation of efforts that looks to redistribute social benefits and burdens through the mechanisms of the state. The growth and power of the state, harnessed toward these ends, not only receive our blessings but are often seen as a certain type of fulfillment of the tradition of Judaism and Christianity.

Daniel Maguire, in *The Moral Core of Judaism and Christianity: Reclaiming the Revolution,* expresses the thoughts of many when he writes that "the distinctive feature of Jewish justice is the stress on redistributive sharing."[3] Because the underclass is quite literally created by the overclass, poverty is appropriately eliminated by "modes of sharing, and the burden of ending poverty falls on the rich."[4] Maguire cautions that genetic studies of influences on modern policies are always difficult, but "these redistributive principles of justice, born in Israel, are a probable influence on Western humanitarian theories of progressive taxing and social-welfare policy."[5] In this framework, government is the prime, though not the only, overseer of the common good.[6]

For John B. Cobb in *Sustaining the Common Good,*[7] reliance on the market model for economic organization promotes laissez-faire, free trade, the mobility of capital, and therefore necessarily leads to the erosion of human communities, the oppression of the poor, and the violation of the environment. Free trade and global interdependence in particular reduce the power of everyone except "the few manipulators of capital" and oppressively "increase the gap between the rich and poor."[8] Cobb spends perilously little space justifying his empirical reading of the global situation as a total and "unmitigated disaster,"[9] and even less space connecting the observed problems in a causal way with free trade and market economics. But in his vision of a new world order, he does call for "decentralizing both political and economic power, always keeping the political power dominant."[10] In this framework also, government is the prime overseer of the common good.

A host of other recent works speak similarly. For Timothy J. Gorringe in *Capital and the Kingdom,* inequality in pay is irrational and morally intolerable.[11] Therefore, the primary sense in which ethics informs economics is to recover a sense of distributive justice.[12] Also for Prentiss Pemberton and Daniel Rush Finn in *Toward a Christian Economic Ethic,* meeting the just entitlements of the poor will involve "a more significant transfer of income from the 'successful' to the poor."[13]

Repeatedly, social justice in pursuit of the common good is substantively elaborated primarily to mean activity by the *federal government* on behalf of those disadvantaged by race, class, and gender.

Of course, the conventional wisdom is really not very different among the more prominent modern day interpreters of Catholic Social Thought[14] who frequently share an inclination to look primarily to state regulation and sometimes even to state ownership of the means of production in order to bring about economic justice. Indeed, some do go so far as to claim that some form of socialism (usually "democratic socialism") seems indicated given the current situation of widespread injustice. David Hollenbach has argued that democratic socialism is "structurally and strategically congruent with the present human situation."[15] Donal Dorr is quite adamant about his rejection of market systems as inherently unjust and his strong preference for socialism. For Dorr, the natural tendency of market forms of economic organization is to "concentrate wealth in the hands of the minority" and to "widen the gap between the rich and the poor."[16] Furthermore, the real-world failures of socialism are excused as unfortunate situations of "bureaucratic mismanagement, corruption and a pandering to various power elites."[17]

In *The Catholic Ethic in American Society,*[18] John E. Tropman argues that the Catholic ethic is characterized by two core concepts: sharing and communalism. He states this thesis as a contrast to the Protestant ethic which is characterized by two different core concepts: achievement and individualism. For Tropman, a culture based on the sharing ethic "begins simply with the concept of sharing to meet social need."[19] For Tropman, the Catholic ethic in principle and practice is tied to the development of the welfare state in this country and in Europe.[20] Tropman consistently associates the rise of Catholic influence with the growth of a welfare state. Therefore, the primary contribution of activists such as John Ryan has been to encourage the ethic of sharing and therefore also the growth of the welfare state, and no departure from this trajectory of things is given serious or extended consideration in his book.

Of course, there are also thinkers, Michael Novak most prominently, whose scholarship takes exception to this broad line of thought. However, aspects of their moral theory remain undeveloped, and they have yet to integrate their moral theory with economic analysis. They also constitute a deliberately marginalized minority. The Catholic Theological Society of America was fortunate to have Jon Sobrino, S.J., address a plenary session at its June 1995 meeting. The following remarks seemed to be accepted as conventional wisdom:[21]

> Neoliberalism has often enough explicated its utopia in terms of the Christian tradition. . . . Michael Novak, theologian of capitalism, says things like these.[22] "For many years one of my favorite texts of Scripture was Isaiah 53:2–3: 'He grew up like a sapling before him, like a shoot from the parched earth. There was in him no stately bearing to make us look at him, nor appearance that would attract us to him. He was spurned and avoided by men, a man of suffering, accustomed to infirmity. One of those from whom men hide their faces, spurned, and we held him in no esteem.' I want to apply those terms to the modern business corporation, an extremely spurned incarnation of the presence of God in this world." If Novak were right, my thesis would be false. But Novak is not right. For anyone who has not lost his common sense and who still has a "heart of flesh," the Third World victims can open up the real totality of this world.

At precisely the correct moment, the listening audience offered the proper "gasp of disapproval" for the misleading and inflammatory quote improperly excised from Novak's work. Even if I considered myself fit to judge such things, I do not feel that the accusations regarding a loss of "common sense" and a "heart of flesh" would be warranted here. Sobrino might have read just a few pages further and quoted less selectively so as to reflect the balanced treatment which Novak gives to the subject:[23]

> Corporations err morally, then, in many ways. They may through their advertising appeal to hedonism and escape, in ways that undercut the restraint and self-discipline required by a responsible democracy and that discourage the deferral of present satisfaction on which savings and investment for the future depend. They may incorporate methods of governance that injure dignity, cooperation, inventiveness, and personal development. They may seek their own immediate

interests at the expense of the common good. They may become improperly involved in the exercise of political power. They may injure the conscience of their managers or workers. They are capable of the sins of individuals and of grave institutional sins as well. Thus, it is a perfectly proper task of all involved within corporations and in society at large to hold them to the highest moral standards, to accuse them when they fail and to be vigilant about every form of abuse.

The truth is that for Novak, the modern corporation is *semper refor-manda*—always in need of reform.[24] Sobrino's own more mainstream perspective is of course strongly antimarket; uses "exploitation" by capital as a central theme; and favors expanded political direction of the economic sector. My reading of his comments is that those who have the audacity to investigate along Novak's lines of thought would also be suspect; i.e., they are likely scholars with no sense and stone hearts. Such scholars would risk the same painful depersonalizing references as is Novak's fate. Without speculating about Sobrino's intentions, the effect at least of his comments would inevitably be intimidation. Nevertheless, it is this mainstream perspective that I must venture to take for honest and critical investigation in this chapter.

To be clear, my alternative perspective which does not emphasize the role of central authorities in the achievement of economic justice and which draws on the resources of Catholic Social Thought is only that: one alternative vision. I do not argue here that this vision is the only vision which can claim support from Catholic Social Thought, since there is a very legitimate pluralism around such matters. Yet I do argue that it is strongly indicated, based on the discussion which follows. Furthermore, while the work does presume and rely on work done from a neoconservative perspective, differences in method and content from Novak's form of neoconservatism are spelled out, especially in chapter 4. Finally, while some (Novak and others) have defended the moral foundations of capitalist economics in light of Catholic Social Thought, no one to the best of my knowledge has done so while integrating systematically economic and empirical analysis.

Such a systematic integration may not only be defended but I think it is actually demanded by any theology that aspires to the name

"Catholic". The Church has explicitly stated that a proper under-standing of the "signs of the times" is a necessary condition for it to carry out its earthly task:

> Inspired by no earthly ambition, the Church seeks but a solitary goal: to carry forward the work of Christ under the lead of the befriending Spirit. . . . To carry out such a task, the Church has always had the duty of scrutinizing the signs of the times and of interpreting them in the light of the Gospel. (*Gaudium et Spes,* par. 3–4)

When Catholic Social Thought speaks to current economic condi-tions, then it cannot avoid interpreting these existing conditions in the development of an appropriate theology. John Coleman, S.J., has stated that "any definite theological position limits the variety of sociological positions compatible with it and vice versa."[25] The ques-tion we must then ask is how well Catholic Social Thought has understood the present state of things and identified the core problems in the achievement of economic justice. If Catholic Social Thought diagnoses the existing situation well, then theological constructs are developed which are more appropriate and useful in achieving eco-nomic justice. I do take the global neoliberal revolution in political economy as an important sign of the times.

Development in Modern Catholic Social Thought

The three ideas that the market system is a poor basis on which to establish justice; that the essential economic problem in a market system is the exploitation of labor by capital; and that the state is chiefly responsible to ensure economic justice may also be found in Catholic Social Thought. However, these ideas undergo significant evolution which has consequently led to the development of very different theological approaches to economic justice.

Responding to the difficult situation of the working classes in the late nineteenth century under early industrial capitalism, the official Church under Pope Leo XIII issued the encyclical letter *Rerum No-varum* (1891). The theological perspective in the document is largely Thomistic, and the perspective offered on modern society is critical.

The encyclical announces its intention to "define the relative rights

and mutual duties of the rich and of the poor, capital and labor."
(*Rerum Novarum,* par. 2) In the document "capital" refers to owners
and is almost synonymous with the rich, while "labor" is used
synonymously with the poor. Leo finds that capital and the state have
not performed their duties with reference to labor. Capital is responsible for the miserable condition of labor, and the *state,* which must
protect economic rights especially of the disadvantaged, has failed to
secure economic rights. The essential conflict then is "capital vs.
labor" with complicity on the part of the state for economic injustice.
The problem can be solved if capital and the state will respect the
legitimate rights of labor to the basic necessities for human flourishing.

Most historians, with good reason, would likely agree that there
was considerable exploitation of labor in the nineteenth century.
However, even this interpretation is subject to qualification. It is not
always easy to distinguish between low levels of productivity and
hence a low standard of living and exploitation. Milton Friedman
makes the point:[26]

> The first myth might be called the robber baron myth. In your courses
> in history, ordinary political history . . . you will have learned that the
> nineteenth century in the United States was an era of rugged, unre-
> strained individualism in which heartless monopoly capitalists ex-
> ploited the poor unmercifully, ground the helpless under their heels,
> and profited at the expense of the rest of the community. . . .
>
>   While the nineteenth century was a period of rugged individual-
> ism, almost every other feature of the myth is false. Far from being
> a period in which the poor were being ground under the heels of the
> rich and exploited unmercifully, there is probably no other period in
> history, in this or any other country, in which the ordinary man had
> as large an increase in his standard of living as in the period between
> the Civil War and the First World War.

I would argue against Friedman that increases in the *material* standard
of living can occur simultaneously with decreases in the quality of life
when other considerations are taken into account such as environ-
mental damage, the existence of child labor, dangerous working conditions, and so forth. Nevertheless, we must reckon with the fact that

economic science has documented that the *rises* in productivity and the consequent (material) standard of living that occurred during the time when Leo promulgated his anticapital message were literally without precedent in previous history.

With the exception of Japan, all advanced industrial countries are European or are offshoots of Europe, and the documented evidence (table 1.1) for these countries shows that the material standard of living measured by the average annual compound growth rates in gross domestic product (GDP) remained roughly unchanged for one thousand years between 500 and 1500 A.D. but has risen dramatically with the advent of merchant capitalism and modern capitalism.[27]

For a more recent example of this dramatic increase in the rate of economic growth, real per capita U.S. GDP in 1989 was seventeen times what is was in 1820. The corresponding rates of increase for other countries are given in table 1.2.[28] These rates of increase stand in exceedingly sharp contrast with the previous *millennium*. It is not unreasonable to question whether the sharp papal condemnations of capitalism are consonant with such basic empirical findings.

Nevertheless, we shall see that by the time of the Great Depression, this belief that capitalistic exploitation was at the heart of modern economic hardship would reach new heights.

Pope Pius XI, seeking to address economically depressed times, issued the encyclical *Quadragesimo Anno* (1931) on the fortieth anniversary of *Rerum Novarum*. Although strongly reaffirming the contents of the earlier encyclical, it seemed necessary to Pius to write

Table 1.1 *Performance Characteristics of Four Epochs*
Average Annual Compound Growth Rates

Type of Economy	Population	GDP (per head)	GDP
Agrarianism, 500–1500	0.1	0.0	0.1
Advancing agrarianism, 1500–1700	0.2	0.1	0.3
Merchant capitalism, 1700–1820	0.4	0.2	0.6
Capitalism, 1820–1980	0.9	1.6	2.5

Table 1.2   GDP per Head of Population 1820–1989 (using 1985 real dollars)

Country	1820	1989	Coefficient of Multiplication 1820–1989
Australia	$ 1,241	$ 13,584	11
Belgium	1,024	12,876	13
France	1,052	13,837	13
Germany	937	13,989	15
Netherlands	1,307	12,737	10
U.K.	1,405	13,468	8
U.S.A.	1,048	18,317	17

again in order to meet the "new needs and changed conditions of our age." (*Quadragesimo Anno,* par. 40) This is a most appropriate reason to issue a new encyclical. Pius is clear about what the cause of the Great Depression is. He writes that the cause of the Great Depression is the concentration of wealth in the hands of a few who "administer according to their own arbitrary will and pleasure." In fact, the situation is described as a dictatorship:

> This dictatorship is being most forcibly exercised by those who, since they hold the money and completely control it, control credit also and rule the lending of money. Hence they regulate the flow, so to speak, of the lifeblood whereby the entire economic system lives, and have so firmly in their grasp the soul, as it were, of economic life that no one can breathe against their will. (*Quadragesimo Anno,* par. 106)

The solution to this dilemma of "monopoly capitalism" involves a major overhaul of capitalism; there should be a system of "corporatism" which involves large associations of employers and employees who collaborate for the common good, especially in setting wages. By corporatism, we may understand Pius to mean a harmonious, non-conflictual integration of capital and labor through the use of vocational groups (organized by industrial sector, not class) like an organism with many parts but, still, *centrally directed by the state.* One can understand how such a participatory system might be a solution to a (perceived) problem of economic dictatorship and excessive centralization of power. Against the overcentralization of power, Pius XI formulates the principle of subsidiarity:

> Just as it is gravely wrong to take from individuals what they can accomplish by their own initiative and industry and give it to the community, so also it is an injustice and at the same time a grave evil and disturbance of right order to assign to a greater and higher association what lesser and subordinate organizations can do. (*Quadragesimo Anno*, par. 79)

It must be pointed out that there is no school of orthodox economic thought that interprets the Great Depression as Pius does here. There is no evidence that the depression had its roots in "economic concentration" and was "caused" by a group of "economic dictators" who profited from the situation by co-opting national income for themselves. Economists have varied positions about whether any significant trend even exists in the degree of U.S. economic concentration in the past century, but less controversial evidence does exist about the distribution of national income between labor and capital and I will present it later in this chapter.

One may safely generalize that most economists today would attribute the depression to insufficient aggregate demand (total spending) on the part of government, households, and businesses.[29] It was under these conditions that Keynesian economics had its origin. Keynes[30] stressed that capitalism is not a system that would necessarily stabilize at a level output and employment that is consistent with full employment of its resources, particularly in the short run. His thinking led to more activist policies on the part of central governments to manage aggregate demand in order to keep fluctuations in unemployment and inflation within tolerable limits. Furthermore, a host of other objectives could be achieved at the same time, including some income equalization.

But this would not be before the time of Pope John XXIII when Catholic Social Thought learned and integrated these insights. Keynes's more pessimistic view of market performance; the orientation of his theory to increasing employment for labor; and the increased role for the state in achieving the economic common good, also provided for in his theory, resonated with the Catholic theological point of view.

For Pope John XXIII, the basic struggle for economic justice seems to be neither a struggle of "labor vs. capital" nor a problem of "economic dictators," but a struggle for a more balanced economic development. This shift in emphasis accompanied a greater confidence in Western economic institutions and practices and a less severe evaluation of the direction of the modern world. John argued for balance in many different ways. He insisted on a balance in the development of the rich and poor nations; a balance within nations concerning employment and remuneration to the factors of production (land, labor, capital) so that the well being of all would be provided for; a balance between the various sectors of the economy (most prominently mentioned are agriculture and industry); and a balanced notion of development to include spiritual as well as material progress. This "fine tuning" was for the most part to be accomplished by the central national political authority.

The duties of the state include the pursuit of such economic balance under its mandate to assist in the achievement of the economic common good through various means:

> These same developments make it possible to keep fluctuations in the economy within bounds, and to provide effective measures for avoiding mass unemployment. Consequently, it is requested again and again of public authorities responsible for the common good, that they intervene in a wide variety of economic affairs, and that, in a more extensive and organized way than heretofore, they adapt institutions, tasks, means, and procedures to this end. (*Mater et Magistra,* par. 54)

This confidence that the state can keep "fluctuations in the economy within bounds," interpreted in the light of the times, is almost certainly a reference to Keynesian economics. The early 1960s was a time of (unparalleled) confidence among many Keynesian economists that the market economy could be fine tuned so as to keep inflation and particularly unemployment at very low levels. The duty to do this then is established here by John. In later documents the experiences of the 1970s and 1980s brought considerable turbulence to macroeconomics and to Catholic social teaching as well; this turbulence changed the perception of the duties of the state in the area of economics. For now at least, Catholic social teaching is very optimistic and confidently adopts a "liberal"[31] program of state intervention.

In the encyclical of Pope Paul VI, *Populorum Progressio* (1967), there is an increasing skepticism about the direction of the modern world. The primary objection is that it does not seem to give attention to the priority of helping the less advantaged persons and especially nations. The optimism of John has been diminished indeed. Paul complains that people today do not understand the proper priorities for economic life. Unlike Pius XI in *Quadragesimo Anno,* there is no theory of monopoly capitalism. Even the softer charge of exploitation by capital as found in *Rerum Novarum* is not pressed. The problem is that people today have accepted technology and progress, and it is correct that they do this, but they have failed to give it adequate direction:

> The world is sick. Its illness consists less in the unproductive monopolization of resources by a small number of men than in the lack of brotherhood among individuals and peoples.
>
> Without abolishing the competitive market, it should be kept within the limits which make it just and moral, and therefore human. (*Populorum Progressio,* par. 66 and 61)

The fact that the modern world has given inadequate direction to economic life has two aspects. According to Paul, the market, when left alone and without state guidance, shows no signs that it will address the situation of the less advantaged. This imbalance creates such disharmony that a more equal development is called "the new name for peace." Furthermore, not only does it not address every person, it does not address the human development of the whole person because it has a stifling materialism which excludes spiritual development. With this lack of community and pursuit of material things, we can say that people have given themselves over to what sociologist Robert Bellah has aptly called "utilitarian individualism."[32] The encyclical is consistent with John's emphasis on the need for a more balanced development; however, the modern world is now seen to be less likely to achieve it. This identification of the economic problem as not consisting in a monopolization of capital but in a lack of sisterhood and brotherhood, that is, a loss in the communitarian spirit and all the evils that this entails, is closer to my own view.

It is also important to note that this document provides no concrete program to solve the ills it has denounced. Since *Quadragesimo Anno,* Catholic Social Thought has generally taken this position. It is necessary for others (with some expertise) who are committed to the values in Catholic social teaching to concern themselves with implementation (which is also a genuinely moral concern).

Octogesima Adveniens, as the title suggests, was written to commemorate the eightieth anniversary of *Rerum Novarum.* The apostolic letter also coincides with the tenth anniversary of *Mater et Magistra* and was promulgated in 1971 by Paul VI. The document's primary emphasis is on the responsibility of Christians to take action to bring about a more just world by combating "flagrant inequalities" in economic, cultural, and political development. The letter begins with an official statement about the above noted recent (after *Quadragesimo Anno*) tendency in Catholic social teaching to avoid giving answers to varied and complex questions:

> In the face of such widely varying situations it is difficult for us to utter a unified message and to put forward a solution which has universal validity. Such is not our ambition, nor is it our mission. It is up to the Christian communities to analyze with objectivity the situation which is proper to their own country, to shed on it the light of the Gospel's unalterable words and to draw principles of reflection, norms of judgment and directives for action from the social teaching of the Church. (*Octogesima Adveniens,* par. 3–4)

Although there is always a working understanding of general economic conditions and problems, the passage indicates an acceptance of the fact of diversity in the situation across cultures and the futility of offering a single solution for all peoples.

The encyclical criticizes a purely "progress" mentality as is so often the error when the economic view of humankind is stressed. Scientific and technological change are seen as tending to promote a new positivism. Such a mentality represents only a partial understanding of the human person, a "partial anthropology." Such a perspective still contains truth, and the sciences which operate on this perspective "are a condition at once indispensable and inadequate for a better discovery of what is human." The modern world needs to dialogue with the Church if all persons are to attain their "full flowering."

As I said earlier, Catholic Social Thought has diagnosed the core problem in achieving economic justice in various ways at various times. We have seen that Catholic Social Thought has experienced critical turning points in its interpretation of the general economic situation and therefore in its theology. At the end of the last century, the problem was largely *capital vs. labor*. The theology developed in response was largely Thomistic, and it understandably stressed the role of the state in setting forth the duties and correlative rights of capital and labor. Forty years later (and during the Great Depression) this understanding gave way to a theory of *monopoly capitalism* and a theology favoring the establishment of a full-fledged Christian social order centrally managed by the state. Of course hardly anyone today would advocate a system of corporatism or understand the depression to have been caused by economic dictators. Yet this severe and highly critical interpretation made such a theology seem reasonable at the time. The next truly major reinterpretation of the economic situation came in the 1960s with the apparent acceptance of some basic tenants of *Keynesian economics* and the importance of fine tuning the economy by the central political authorities in order to meet human needs. Pope Paul VI began a gradual recasting of John's interpretation. Paul adds considerable pessimism about whether the economic situation was really becoming more just. He notes the gross disparities in the distribution of income, and therefore benefits, within societies and between societies/nations, but "capital" does not appear as the principle cause of this misery. Finally, the tendency explicitly mentioned in *Octogesima Adveniens* not to offer specific programs for reform coexists with the need to make general assessments about economics.

We see that Catholic Social Thought has historically had a "working economics" and has made general judgments about the core problems involved in the achievement of economic justice. The social teachings have been critical of market systems and have tended to emphasize the role of the state in the achievement of economic justice. We move now to the present in order to examine the broad assumptions made by John Paul II.

The encyclicals of Pope John Paul II are especially interesting for us because they are more recent in time and because of their Christian Personalist approach. This approach to persons in society attempts to reach a balance between the individualism of Western society and the collectivism of Marxist theory and practice. Personalism affirms the sociality of the human person (against individualism) while insisting on the transcendent value of each individual in society (against Marxism). This perspective is evident in *Laborem Exercens* as John Paul acknowledges the social nature of work today and insists that the rights of workers must receive priority over the systems in which workers participate.

Laborem Exercens was issued in 1981 by John Paul II on the ninetieth anniversary of *Rerum Novarum*. In *Laborem Exercens* John Paul clearly puts forth an understanding of the economic situation and creatively develops his theology. We do well here to review this document carefully.

The letter begins with an introduction emphasizing three points: the significance of work, the reality of changing historical circumstances, and the theological mission of the Church. For John Paul II, work is the key to the social question. He wishes for the Church to widen its horizon and to take in theological questions concerning the whole world. John Paul wishes to stand in the long tradition of Catholic Social Thought since *Rerum Novarum,* but to speak an updated and worldwide message. A focus on labor is thought to be able to deliver a modern and worldwide message. The pursuit of the social goals of peace and justice in the world requires attention to the "labor question."

The second section begins by offering the theological foundations for the letter. The human person is the "image of God partly through the mandate received from his Creator to subdue, to dominate, the earth." This text speaks to us today even in the face of accelerated changes. All persons, in one way or the other, receive a certain dignity by being "workers" who take part in this process of subduing the earth.

Work exists in an objective and in a subjective sense. Work in an objective sense is obtaining from the earth what is necessary for life and the transforming of the earth for our human purposes. Technology is quite naturally an ally for people here, except when it seems to take employment away from some or in any other way injures people. Technology is also part of human dominion over nature:

> If the biblical words "subdue the earth" addressed to man from the very beginning are understood in the context of the whole modern age, industrial and postindustrial, then they undoubtedly include also a relationship with technology, with the world of machinery which is the fruit of the work of the human intellect and an historical confirmation of man's dominion over nature. (*Laborem Exercens,* par. 5)

Work in the subjective sense refers more immediately to the persons doing the work and affected by the work. A person is a "subjective being capable of acting in a planned and rational way, capable of deciding about himself and with a tendency to self-realization." The climax of this section is that the subjective side of work is to have priority over the objective side. So it is wrong to divide people into classes on the basis of the kind of work that they do; and clearly, work is for people, not people for work.

There are threats to this proper order. The chief threat is when the worker is treated as a kind of commodity and not as a true subject in the image of God. Such errors, labeled "capitalism," are understood as an economic system that gives primary importance to the objective side of human work. So capitalism is given a primarily pejorative interpretation.

The response by workers to such mistreatment must be one of solidarity. Of course, one thinks immediately of Poland at this point. "Solidarity" seems to be an alternative to "class struggle" as in Marxism. "Solidarity" in the writing of John Paul II does not have the same overtones of violence and the glorification of a single class implied by the Marxist concept of "class struggle." This subjective side of work not only has personal dimensions, but it is also linked to the family and the nation. Work is also a condition for the possibility of the flourishing of one's family and nation.

In section three we have a discussion about the present conflict between labor and capital. It has always been the teaching of the Church that labor should have priority over capital. Labor is the primary efficient cause and capital is only the instrumental cause of production (in fact, capital is simply the "result of past labor"). People must have priority over things, but this priority is violated by the error of economism which considers human labor solely according to its economic purpose. We see this materialist error in Western capitalism and in the theory of Marxist dialectical materialism. The origins of the problem stem from eighteenth century economic theory and practice. In that time, according to John Paul, capital was set up (unnaturally) against labor and the few capitalists were able to use their superior bargaining power to hold wages down:

> I must however first touch on a very important field of questions in which its [the Church's] teaching has taken shape in this latest period, the one marked and in a sense symbolized by the publication of the encyclical "*Rerum Novarum.*" Throughout this period, which is by no means over, the issue of work has of course been posed on the basis of the great conflict that in the age of and together with industrial development emerged between "capital" and "labor," that is to say between the small but highly influential group of entrepreneurs, owners or holders of the means of production, and the broader multitude of people who lacked these means and who shared in the process of production solely by their labor. The conflict originated in the fact that the workers put their powers at the disposal of the entrepreneurs, and these, following the principle of maximum profit, tried to establish the lowest possible wages for the work done by the employees. In addition there were other elements of exploitation connected with the lack of safety at work and of safeguards regarding the health and living conditions of the workers and their families. (*Laborem Exercens,* par. 11)

John Paul uses a basically philosophical, not an empirical, argument here to establish the existence of exploitation which consists mainly in insufficient wages paid to labor.

Section four explicitly discusses the rights of workers in a system that gives priority to labor. The rights of workers are said to include first of all employment and just remuneration, and also health care, rest, pensions, and safe working conditions. Unions are thought to be helpful in attaining these rights. Unions are not, however, to "play politics." Given the fact of interdependence among nations, we must be sure that relationships are regulated by justice. The growing gap between the rich and poor nations is deplorable.

To conclude, we may say that John Paul saw the basic economic problem as a deficiency in the intended harmony between capital and labor. I agree with Gregory Baum when he summarizes the encyclical:[33]

> *Laborem Exercens* is in accord with liberation theology and political theology in its analysis of the principal cause of misery in the modern world; it is the domination of capital over labor. . . . For both (the East and West) the struggle for a more truly human order, carried on principally by the oppressed and supported by all those who love justice, aims at making capital serve labor, at putting the wealth produced at the service of the workers.

Baum is correct, I think, in his summarization of John Paul's reading in 1981 of modern economics, and furthermore Baum agrees with this reading. However, below I will offer criticisms of this reading and suggest appropriate revisions. It is important to note that the substantiation and background given by John Paul for his thesis that the essential economic problem is the exploitation of labor in a system that gives priority to capital is an argument made on a philosophical level.

There are no concrete economic proposals in this letter. What seems most important is that there be a just order animated by the priority of labor. The subjective side of work, which concerns self, family, and nation, has priority over the objective side. Therefore wages must always be just, ownership of property must serve the universal destination of all goods, the common good, and unions are necessary as a voice for labor.

An assessment about the signs of the times cannot be based on what is at heart a philosophical argument; the philosophical arguments about how labor can be exploited do not circumvent the need for an analysis of the empirical situation to determine if this is in fact the case and if this should serve as the basis for a theology. *Laborem Exercens* has offered familiar arguments establishing only the plausibility of such exploitation. In order to judge the applicability of *Laborem Exercens* with reference to the U.S. economy, it would be important to know what the relative position today of capital and labor is in the United States. Many factors would have to be taken into consideration to make such a judgment, and then it would be difficult to weigh such factors. Fortunately, we can turn to *Laborem Exercens* for guidance here. John Paul says clearly that "in the context of the present there is no more important way for securing a just relationship between the worker and the employer than that constituted by remuneration for work." (par. 19) I will use wages and income here as a sort of index by which to gauge the relative position of capital and labor. Furthermore, although the wage issue will not be the only issue in a discussion about a just relationship between the worker and the employer, it is the most important single factor and other issues concerning the treatment of labor will likely be closely correlated with it.

As is shown in table 1.3, it is most certainly the case that real per capita gross domestic product[34] in the United States has risen steadily and sharply in recent history.

However, we cannot be content to ask if the total economic pie has grown. Our interest requires information about how this output is actually distributed.

Table 1.4 is the work of Irving Kravis.[35] It contains data about the "functional distribution of income," or the distributive shares of national income going to wages and salaries, entrepreneurial income, corporate profits, interest (the return to money capital), and rent (the

Table 1.3   Per Capita Gross Domestic Product (GDP) in Constant Dollars (billions of 1987 dollars)

Year	GDP	Year	GDP
1929	$6,743	1965	$12,712
1930	$6,079	1970	$14,013
1940	$6,857	1975	$14,917
1945	$11,453	1980	$16,584
1950	$9,352	1985	$17,944
1955	$10,699	1990	$19,593
1960	$10,903	1993	$19,888

Source: *Statistical Abstract of the United States,* U.S. Department of Commerce, Bureau of the Census, 1994. Table no. 691.

Table 1.4   Distributive Shares in U.S. National Income

Decade	Wages and Salaries	Entrepr. Income	Corporate Profits	Interest	Rent
1900–1909	55.00%	23.70%	6.80%	5.50%	9.0%
1910–1919	53.60%	23.80%	9.10%	5.40%	8.1%
1920–1929	60.00%	17.50%	7.80%	6.20%	7.7%
1930–1939	67.50%	14.80%	4.00%	8.70%	5.0%
1939–1948	64.60%	17.20%	11.90%	3.10%	3.3%
1949–1958	67.30%	13.90%	12.50%	2.90%	3.4%
1954–1963	69.90%	11.90%	11.20%	4.00%	3.0%
1963–1970	71.70%	9.60%	12.10%	3.50%	3.2%
1971–1981	75.90%	7.10%	8.40%	6.40%	2.2%
1982–1988	73.80%	6.80%	8.60%	9.80%	1.1%

return to property resources). For our purposes we must group the sources of income into just two categories: labor and capital. Labor would seem to include just wages and salaries, and under that assumption it would appear that labor has made steady gains since the turn of the century.

However, it may be more accurate to include entrepreneurial income as "labor" for our purposes. Kravis states:

The bulk of the increase in the share of employee compensation came at the expense of entrepreneurial income. . . .

The long run rise in the employee share and the decline in the entrepreneurial share of income reflect two other important and interrelated trends in the nation's economic structure—the change from an agricultural to an industrial country and the shift out of self-employment into wage and salary employment. The proportion of persons engaged in agriculture declined from more than half of the work force in 1870 to less than 40 percent at the turn of the century, and to 7 percent in the early 1960s, while the proportion of wage and salary employees rose from 58 percent in 1870 to 64 percent at the turn of the century, and to about 85 percent in the 1960s.

So wages and salaries have increased at the expense of entrepreneurial income primarily because individuals who operated a small business or farm some fifty years ago are managers in corporations receiving a salary today. We will include wages and salaries and entrepreneurial income in our measure of "labor" income. Our measure of income to "capital" will be the sum of all income received from property resources. This is the sum of the remaining columns which are corporate profits, interest, and rent.

Even if we accept this second set of data (table 1.5) which construes the time trend more pessimistically from the perspective of labor, we see that the relative shares of national income going to labor and capital have been relatively constant over this century. Furthermore, labor receives a fairly constant 80 percent of all income. Although by today's standards the level of wages at the turn of the century was miserably low, we can attribute this primarily to low productivity. It would be incorrect to assert that changes in the degree of exploitation are responsible for wage gains when one compares the wage situation then with the wage situation now.

We have now looked at this question of income distribution from a number of perspectives. James Gustafson has stated that theology cannot "be incongruous with well established data and explanatory principles established by relevant sciences, and must be in some way indicated by these."[36] The data above help define the broad terrain and give us a basic perspective on the distribution of income within

Table 1.5   *Distributive Shares in U.S. National Income Going to Labor and Capital*

Decade	Total Labor	Total Capital
1900–1909	78.70%	21.30%
1910–1919	77.40%	22.60%
1920–1929	77.50%	21.70%
1930–1939	82.30%	17.70%
1939–1948	81.80%	18.30%
1949–1958	81.20%	18.80%
1954–1963	81.80%	18.20%
1963–1970	81.30%	18.80%
1971–1981	83.00%	17.00%
1982–1988	80.60%	19.40%

U.S. capitalism. It does seem to me that the theology in *Laborem Exercens* is incongruous with these well-established data.

This classic critique by John Paul became popular with the Marxist "labor theory of value" according to which the value of a commodity depends only on the amount of labor required to produce the commodity. Profits are possible only because labor is paid less than the value of what it produces (hence also the existence of exploitation). Of course, modern market economics rejects the labor theory of value, arguing that in the process of production, resources of land, labor, capital, and entrepreneurial ability all contribute to the value of a commodity and require remuneration. Furthermore, the value of a commodity will fluctuate in the market based on factors that impact supply and demand; it is not helpful to speak of a timeless and stable intrinsic "value" of a commodity determined by the labor hours included in its creation. The scientific support for this critique is in all ways lacking; we would do better to look at the dramatically unequal distribution of labor income itself than to continue to cling to the capital vs. labor dialectic.

John Paul himself suggested that this issue of exploitation turned most principally on the wage issue. Therefore I have assessed his thesis of exploitation on criteria that are internal to his own thinking. It seems that theology concerned with work and economic justice that is informed by basic trends in the U.S. economy would likely not identify the major problem as "capital vs. labor." Although good reasons may be (and often are) given for a redistribution of income from capital to labor, most income is and has always been received by labor, and any significant reform of the distribution of income must redistribute primarily labor income. The vast differences in the wages and salaries received by accountants, maids, doctors, nurses, farm laborers, teachers, waitresses, and lawyers bear the brunt of responsibility for distributive injustice; and from this we see the lack of solidarity within labor. Economic justice cannot come to the United States solely through a relatively painless redistribution of income from capital to labor.

I have come to believe that the most recent encyclical, *Centesimus Annus,* breaks important new ground. John Paul uses his Christian Personalism to offer us creative recombinations of well-established ideas about solidarity, private property, the common good, subsidiarity, human dignity, and so forth. Once again, I will concentrate on the methodological issues that have concerned us so far and on the understanding as presented by the encyclical of the core problem involved in achieving economic justice.

We find confirmation of the methodological principle enunciated some time ago by John Coleman that "any definite theological position limits the variety of sociological positions compatible with it and vice versa." John Paul writes:

> But pastoral solicitude also prompts me to propose *an analysis of some events of recent history*. It goes without saying that part of the responsibility of Pastors is to give careful consideration to current events in order to discern the new requirements of evangelization. However, such an analysis is not meant to pass definitive judgments since this does not fall *per se* within the Magisterium's specific domain. (*Centesimus Annus,* par. 3; italics in the original)

The need for sociological study is accepted here, and there is a more or less open door to the sort of criticism in which we have engaged above.

Furthermore, the real necessity actually to *assimilate* sociological study into a theology receives explicit attention:

> In addition, the Church's social teaching has an important interdisciplinary dimension. In order better to incarnate the one truth about man in different and constantly changing social, economic and political contexts, this teaching enters into dialogue with the various disciplines concerned with man. It assimilates what these disciplines have to contribute, and helps them to open themselves to a broader horizon, aimed at serving the individual person who is acknowledged and loved in the fullness of his or her vocation. (*Centesimus Annus,* par. 59)

This perspective forces John Paul to give great attention to contemporary events, including those happening in eastern Europe at the time, and to the social sciences (including economics) which interpret these events.

There is continuity with previous teaching in this encyclical. The letter begins with a review of *Rerum Novarum* and the situation which it criticized. The conflict between capital and labor was the locus of injustice, and it gave rise to the horrendously low wages of the time. Today there are still some "instances" of this struggle. (*Centesimus Annus,* par. 8) However, to say there are instances of this struggle is quite a long way from using the struggle as a centerpiece of theology as was the case in *Laborem Exercens.*

In *Centesimus Annus* are strong denunciations of the two extremes of centralized bureaucratic planning and unrestrained capitalism, since these do not guarantee the dignity of the human person. Gone, however, is an understanding of the core problem of economic injustice as the exploitation of the many workers by the (fewer in number, and sometimes monopoly) capitalists. In fact, it is no longer the ownership of capital but the possession of technology and education that is the decisive factor in production. (*Centesimus Annus,* par. 32) This emphasis encourages a shift in focus to the various categories of labor in an analysis of economic power.

Certainly gone is a definition of capitalism that is primarily pejorative (this was the case in *Laborem Exercens*). Capitalism, *circumscribed within a strong juridical framework,* should actually be the goal of countries now making efforts to rebuild their economic systems (formerly the Eastern bloc) and for countries of the third world. (*Centesimus Annus,* par. 42) Capitalism has the important advantage of efficiency, and it could be yet more efficient if it would only take more seriously those rights which it continues to neglect. (*Centesimus Annus,* par. 34–35)[37]

The Christian Personalist perspective of John Paul reaffirms what has become the guiding principle of Catholic Social Thought: the dignity of the human person. It is the Church that has a correct view of the human person. Indeed, it is here that the Church makes its specific contribution:

> The way in which he is involved in building his own future depends on the understanding he has of himself and of his own destiny. It is on this level that *the Church's specific and decisive contribution to true culture* is to be found. (*Centesimus Annus,* par. 11; italics in the original)

In service then of the dignity of the human person, certain principles have come to light in Catholic Social Thought and are once again reaffirmed by John Paul II. Important among these principles are the need for the Gospel if any genuine solution to the social question is to be found, limitations on the right to private property and the universal destination of the earth's goods, the principle of subsidiarity, the existence of economic rights to a just wage, to organization in solidarity, and to economic participation on the part of workers.

It seems that John Paul now embraces a form of the welfare state as the most promising option. Clearly the welfare state does not represent laissez faire capitalism. However, such welfare state functions should be pursued only to the extent that the welfare state does not become a "social assistance state" by intervening excessively in economic life, depriving society of its proper responsibilities. There are well-defined roles for the state which include:

1. "[G]uarantees of individual freedom and private property, as well as a stable currency and efficient public services . . ."
2. "[O]verseeing and directing the exercise of human rights in the economic sector . . . the State has a duty to sustain business activities by creating conditions which will ensure job opportunities, by stimulating those activities where they are lacking or by supporting them in moments of crisis . . ."
3. "The state has the further right to intervene when particular monopolies create delays or obstacles to development." (*Centesimus Annus,* par. 48)

John Paul has truly assumed the position of a "friendly critic" with respect to the market. While insisting on the shortcomings of market society, he shares a basic understanding about how the system does meet human needs with the aid of state intervention. Orthodox economics produces an almost identical list of legitimate economic functions for the state.[38]

It would certainly be instructive to view the generally superior growth of developing and advanced economies in Europe, the Americas, Asia, and Africa which are market economies and not oppressed by excessive regulation by central governments. However, the question would still remain: what can we say about the poor in those countries? That is likely the single most significant moral question. Comprehensive statistical comparisons of precisely that sort would be difficult to come by. However, in order to reinforce this new direction of John Paul II, and to make the worldwide adoption of market systems at least more comprehensible from the moral perspective, I can indeed offer one final statistical argument in this chapter.

The collapse of the Soviet Union and the demise of its satellite system of smaller nations cries out now for analysis and some preliminary statement about the socialist project. This is after all the context in which *Centesimus Annus* was written.

Data on how income is distributed among households in Western nations when compared to the now defunct Soviet Union is very informative and challenges long-held myths. Abram Bergson has done pioneering work in the area of comparative national income distributions. Bergson[39] specifies the income shares, including transfer receipts and earned income of selected percentile groups and the Gini coefficients (see table 1.6).

The table is read as follows: Using the United States as an example, in 1972 the lowest 20 percent of the households received 5.5 percent of the total income, while the highest 10 percent received 28.6 percent. These figures tend to show less income inequality in the USSR than actually existed. Bergson states that figures for income inequality would increase if data were available which included rural households in the Soviet statistics. It is also true that taxes bring a degree of equalization in income in Western countries.

Table 1.6   Income Shares of Selected Percentile Groups and Gini Coefficients

Country and Year	GDP per cap. (U.S.=100)	10% Lowest	20%	20%	10% Highest	Gini Coefficient
Urban households, post-tax:						
USSR, 1972–74	48	3.4	8.7	38.5	24.1	.288
All households, pre-tax:						
U.K. 1973	66	3.5	8.3	39.9	23.9	.308
France 1970	68	2	5.8	47.2	31.8	.398
Canada 1969	74	2.2	6.2	43.6	27.8	.363
U.S. 1972	99	1.8	5.5	44.4	28.6	.376
Sweden 1972	80	3.5	9.3	35.2	20.5	.254

The Gini coefficient is a measure of income inequality. The larger the number, the larger the degree of income inequality. In a careful analysis, Bergson draws these conclusions:[40]

> In sum, any definitive judgment on comparative income inequality in the USSR and the West is obviously excluded, but Soviet income inequality probably has been found to be greater than often supposed. It is very possibly as great as or greater than that of Sweden, and not much less than that in some other Western countries such as Norway and the United Kingdom. Income inequality in the USSR is commonly assumed to be less than that in the US. That is doubtless so, though not by as wide a margin as sometimes imagined.

Definitive comparisons remain impossible because of the incomplete nature of the available data and because of the inherent difficulty in making these international comparisons. Yet, in an examination of the after-tax and transfer income of the bottom 20 percent to index the situation of the socially disadvantaged or the "poor," we see that the poor of the Soviet Union fare worse than the poor of the United States in an absolute sense. Although the relative share of income of this group is higher in the Soviet Union (8.7 percent excluding the rural sector versus 5.5 percent in the United States), the far higher GDP base in the United States more than offsets this advantage by being slightly more than twice as high as that in the Soviet Union. *The likely conclusion is that the human needs of virtually all segments of society are better satisfied under market systems.*

This analysis still leaves open a wide road with respect to the sort of market economy that one might reasonably favor. Market arrangements, social conditions, and outcomes vary significantly for France, the United States, Canada, and for more homogeneous countries such as Sweden. In the chapters that follow, I focus on the case and appropriate moral agenda for the United States in light of its recent economic history.

Where does this leave us today in terms of Catholic Social Thought? Exploitation by capital is not the major problem (*Rerum Novarum, Laborem Exercens*), monopoly capitalism is certainly not the general rule (*Quadragesimo Anno*), nor is the economic problem largely a question of *state* directed fine tuning of things (*Mater et Magistra*).

According to John Paul II in *Centesimus Annus,* it is certainly true that capitalism is a system upon which we can build for greater justice. John Paul has also expanded the application of the principle of subsidiarity through his explicit development of the concept of the "social assistance state." Over the sweep of one century, the social teachings have come to a more positive understanding of market systems; the teachings have moved well beyond the capital-labor dialectic; and the teachings are much more cautious about an excessive role for the state in the achievement of economic justice. We have seen here economic data that support these three developments in basic perspective. At the start of this chapter, I stated that social ethics today should show a more serious reading and creative moral exploration of market political economies. The Christian Personalism of John Paul is a strong beginning in this direction. This includes an awareness of the moral and economic dangers of an excessive presence of the state in economic life.

Conclusion: Three Ideas Wrong

To conclude, the three presuppositions discussed earlier no longer define Catholic Social Thought. Market systems are not seen as a poor basis on which to meet human needs; the essential economic problem in a market system is not the exploitation of labor by capital; and justice does not necessarily require the state to expand its role in economic life. This chapter has not attempted to offer a definitive statement about the relative merits of market and nonmarket systems. I have, however, tried to show the developments in interpretation that have taken place in Catholic Social Thought and to indicate the empirical support for the same.

Let me also state that the focus of this chapter has been restricted to certain issues which are important for the purpose of this work. My attempt has not been to demonstrate the continuities which surely do exist, or to show how the early documents developed ideas of lasting value for the tradition. In many ways the present teachings may be seen as creative recombinations of well-established ideas about private property, the common good, subsidiarity, human dignity, and so forth. I have also avoided speculations as to why Catholic Social Thought engaged in such heavy critique of the market which was only adjusted in more recent decades. It seems likely that the heavy critique was at least related to its sense of alienation from modernity in general, particularly prior to Vatican II. The Church of course remained strongly tied to tradition, authority, and other values which the market frequently undermined. Instead, I have focused on the market-related arguments themselves which are at issue for our purposes. Others may well want to examine Catholic Social Thought differently; not so much as having made certain above-mentioned errors in economic analysis, but as a problem in basic perspective and a consequent dismissive approach toward the market.

For those who would agree that there is a moral order and that violation of this moral order has negative consequences and acting in harmony with it has positive consequences, it would be impossible for the productivity and relative success of market systems to be devoid of moral underpinning. Later chapters are devoted to the development of a Personalist moral theory which recognizes and cherishes the moral insights incorporated into the market system of Western liberalism. Presuming the existence of the current system, the moral theory will also offer constructive critique and set an appropriate moral agenda for those who would pursue "social justice." This moral theory takes American capitalism as an acceptable starting point on which to advance the cause of justice. But first, before setting a vision and determining where we must go, it is necessary to have even more of a sense of where we have recently been, where we are, and what we have learned.

Notes

1. Richard John Neuhaus, *The Naked Public Square* (Grand Rapids, Michigan: William B. Eerdmans Publishing Co., 1984), p.207.
2. Neuhaus, *The Naked Public Square,* p.231.
3. Daniel C. Maguire, *The Moral Core of Judaism and Christianity: Reclaiming the Revolution* (Minneapolis: Fortress Press, 1993), p.133.
4. Maguire, *The Moral Core of Judaism and Christianity,* p.135.
5. Maguire, *The Moral Core of Judaism and Christianity,* p.142.
6. Maguire, *The Moral Core of Judaism and Christianity,* p.161.
7. John B. Cobb, Jr., *Sustaining the Common Good: A Christian Perspective on the Global Economy* (Cleveland, Ohio: The Pilgrim Press, 1994).

8. Cobb, *Sustaining the Common Good*, p.42.
9. Cobb, *Sustaining the Common Good*, p.130.
10. Cobb, *Sustaining the Common Good*, p.121.
11. Timothy J. Gorringe, *Capital and the Kingdom: Theological Ethics and Economic Order* (Maryknoll, New York: Orbis Press, 1994), p.111.
12. Timothy J. Gorringe, *Capital and the Kingdom*, pp.41–2.
13. Prentiss Pemberton and Daniel Rush Finn, *Toward a Christian Economic Ethic: Stewardship and Social Power* (Minneapolis: Winston Press, 1985), p.181.
14. There is a wealth of papal and conciliar documents which could potentially fall under the heading of Catholic Social Thought. With few exceptions, I will generally focus my analysis here on those documents which, it is generally agreed, have done the most to define this tradition. These include *Rerum Novarum* (Leo XIII, 1891), *Quadragesimo Anno* (Pius XI, 1931), *Mater et Magistra* (John XXIII, 1961), *Pacem in Terris* (John XXIII, 1963), *Gaudium et Spes* (Second Vatican Council), *Populorum Progressio* (Paul VI, 1967), *Octogesima Adveniens* (Paul VI, 1971), *Justice in the World* (Synod of Bishops, 1971), *Laborem Exercens* (John Paul II, 1981), *Sollicitudo Rei Socialis* (John Paul II, 1987), and *Centesimus Annus* (John Paul II, 1991). Because I write in the context of the United States, I will also make reference to U.S. episcopal teaching.
15. David Hollenbach, *Claims in Conflict, Retrieving and Renewing the Catholic Human Rights Tradition* (New York: Paulist Press, 1979), p.195.
16. Donal Dorr, *Option for the Poor* (Maryknoll, New York: Orbis Press, 1992), p.121.
17. Dorr, *Option for the Poor* p.121.
18. John E. Tropman, *The Catholic Ethic in American Society* (San Francisco: Jossey-Bass Publishers, 1994).
19. Tropman, *The Catholic Ethic*, p.186.
20. Tropman, *The Catholic Ethic*, pp.130, 162.
21. Paul Crowley, editor, *The Catholic Theological Society of America: Proceeding of the Fiftieth Annual Convention*, vol. 50, June 1995, p.74.
22. Sobrino takes this quote from Michael Novak, *Toward a Theology of the Corporation*, (Washington and London: American Enterprise Institute for Public Policy Research, 1981), p.33.
23. Novak, *Toward a Theology of the Corporation*, p.51.
24. Novak, *Toward a Theology of the Corporation*, p.43.
25. John Coleman, "A Response to Andrew Greeley," from the *Proceedings of the Catholic Theological Society of America*, 1977.

26. Milton Friedman, *Bright Promises, Dismal Performance—An Economist's Protest* (San Diego: Harcourt Brace Jovanovich, 1983).

27. Angus Maddison, *Phases of Capitalist Development* (New York: Oxford University Press, 1988), p.6.

28. Angus Maddison, *Dynamic Forces in Capitalist Development* (New York: Oxford University Press, 1991), pp.6–7.

29. This is course a Keynesian statement of the problem. The monetarist would focus on the decline of the money supply (and only then the consequent decline in aggregate spending) which fell by one-third between 1929 and 1933 even though the Federal Reserve had the ability to prevent this.

30. John Maynard Keynes published his *General Theory of Employment, Interest and Money* in 1936. The book revolutionized economic theory.

31. At the time such attempts at fine tuning the economy were particularly associated with the Democratic Party in the United States. John incurred the wrath of many conservatives as is typified by William F. Buckley's famous statement in the *National Review,* "Mater si, Magistra no."

32. Robert Bellah, et al., *Habits of the Heart* (New York: Harper & Row, 1985).

33. Gregory Baum, *The Priority of Labor* (New York: Paulist Press, 1982), p.76.

34. Gross domestic product is the economic output produced within the geographical area of the nation in a given year. "Per capita" simply indicates that this figure has been divided by the number of resident persons, while "real" indicates that the figure has been adjusted for inflation using some base year (1987 in this case).

35. Irving Kravis, "Income Distribution: Functional Share," *International Encyclopedia of Social Science* (New York: Macmillan Publishing Co. and Free Press, 1968), vol. 7, p.134, updated.

36. James Gustafson, *Ethics from a Theocentric Perspective* (Chicago: University of Chicago Press, 1981), vol. 1.

37. Whether this harmony between efficiency and rights is a noble lie or actually the case is a question I would leave open. It may well be the case that meeting rights reduces the material standard of living while raising the larger "quality of life." In any case, this sort of argument is common and popular in business ethics.

38. It might be interesting to show this by taking one of the most popular economic text books in the United States as an example: *Macroeconomics* (McConnell, 1990) contains a chapter entitled, "The Economic Functions of Government" (ch.6). Five such functions are listed:

1. Provide the legal foundation and framework for the price system.
2. Maintain competition in the private sector.
3. Redistribute income.
4. Reallocate resources.
5. Stabilize the economy.

Economic function 1 for McConnell is contained in 1 for John Paul; economic function 2 for McConnell is contained in 3 for John Paul; function 3 for McConnell is contained in 2 for John Paul; and economic function 5 for McConnell is contained in 2 for John Paul. Number 4 for McConnell refers to the need to curb the production of goods which entail spillover costs (such as pollution) and the need to promote the production of goods which entail spillover benefits (such as education) in order to achieve an optimal allocation of resources in a market economy. This is not (explicitly) covered by John Paul since he is quite naturally less concerned with the technicalities of optimization theory.

39. Abram Bergson, "Income Inequality Under Soviet Socialism," in *Journal of Economic Literature,* vol. 22, September 1984, pp.1052–99.
40. Bergson, "Income Inequality Under Soviet Socialism," p.1073.

2

The Moral Imperative: A Redistributionist State

> I ask, how can God's love survive in a man who has enough
> of this world's goods yet closes his heart to his brother when
> he sees him in need? — 1 John 3:17

Although American capitalism has been fabulously productive, a very obvious moral agenda still remains in the twentieth century. Given the continued presence of large inequalities in income and wealth, there must be more progress made in the area of "distributive justice." More than any other thinker, this perspective was forged within Catholicism by Father John Ryan (d.1945). Ryan's synthesis of ethics and economics remains unsurpassed even today, and his basic framework actually remains dominant in American Catholic episcopal statements. I will show why this synthesis has spent its force and indicate why we must move beyond it. Of course, a serious moral argument must have a strong foundation in the history and facts of the issue, therefore some economic detail necessarily accompanies this chapter.

Keynes and Catholicism: Mr. Right Reverend New Dealer

Michael John Ryan was the first-born child in a family of eleven children.[1] He was born in 1869 to deeply religious Irish Catholic immigrant parents. During John's formative years his family survived as farm workers in Minnesota during very difficult times. John would frequently hear attacks against "Big Business," and especially the railroad, which bore the brunt of populist criticism during hard economic times.

In 1887 John entered St. Thomas Seminary. While in college he learned of the controversy between the Catholic conservatives and liberals. Put briefly, the liberals favored reconciling their faith with the surrounding American culture, while the conservatives tended to hold themselves more aloof. Ryan wished to combine his Catholicism with his Americanism, and consequently his sympathies were with the liberals.[2] Although it is unlikely that Ryan ever read the work of Troeltsch, Ryan's perspective was a "church" and not a "sectarian" one.

Rerum Novarum (1891), the social encyclical of Leo XIII, confirmed Ryan in his social concerns and gave him additional basis to seek the reform of the economic order according to natural law principles. Furthermore, the encyclical prompted the seminary to require students, including Ryan, to study courses in economics and sociology. Again, later during his time as a graduate student at the Catholic University of America, he was influenced by his major professor, Father Bouquillon, whose method was first to investigate the economics and sociology of a problem before making moral judgments.

John Ryan became the best-known American Catholic social ethicist in the early twentieth century and the principal official Catholic spokesperson for progressive social change.[3] Many of his ideas became part of the U.S. economic debate, especially as they were incorporated into the American "Bishops Program of Social Reconstruction" (1919). Ryan's economics was sound; indeed his economics may be and was described as "New Deal" in orientation and was most appropriate to its time.

Ryan aligned himself in important ways with the tradition of Jean Sismondi, Thomas Malthus, and John Maynard Keynes who felt the key to economic health was the level of total spending—which is given by the sum of household, business, government, and foreign spending for domestic goods and services (called "aggregate demand"). This allowed Ryan to demonstrate a real harmony between good economics (what leads to higher output and employment) and the key demand of his natural law ethics (a family living wage): business activity could be resuscitated by supplementing aggregate demand which could be done by increasing the spending power of working class households. This was the "pump priming" of Franklin Delano Roosevelt's New Deal. In economics, the theoretical framework for such government interventions was laid by John Maynard Keynes.[4]

John Ryan's work *Distributive Justice*,[5] represents an interesting combination of market economics and a natural law theory applied to the problem of income distribution in the United States. In *Distributive Justice* Ryan asserts labor's right to a living wage, and he justifies the income received by the factors of production other than labor. Ryan prioritizes all these income returns (to labor and nonlabor sources) from a moral perspective. Ryan divides his discussion of income into traditional economic categories. He examines the returns to the four factors of production: land, capital, entrepreneurial ability, and labor. The returns to these factors are rent, interest, profit, and wages respectively. In his discussions of land and capital he does include a brief justification of capitalism based on its efficiency compared with alternative systems; he does not justify capitalism on any intrinsic or metaphysical grounds.[6]

John Ryan claimed that private property (here meaning ownership of the means of production) and the payment of rent are morally acceptable largely because such a system is much more efficient than the main alternative which is socialism. It is very probably superior to the single-tax system also. Under single tax, the government would confiscate not the land, but only the rent associated with the land. However, such a system would certainly produce vast inefficiencies and inequities. Private property is only considered an indirect right because it is expedient and superior to the alternatives: private ownership is not only socially preferable to the socialist and the single-tax systems of land tenure, but it is, as compared with socialism certainly, and as compared with the single tax probably, among man's natural rights.[7]

Ryan is unable to find any intrinsic justification for taking interest on capital except for the case when a capitalist has sacrificed to save and therefore deserves interest on the amount concerned. The state is, however, justified in allowing interest because the practical difficulties in doing otherwise are insurmountable. Capitalists are allowed to take interest because they have the best presumptive title based on the industrial system. Nevertheless, this claim to interest is weaker than the worker's claim to a living wage.

Profits as a return to the entrepreneur are required by our economic system and are therefore moral in light of the alternative (i.e., socialism). There is no right to a minimum profit by business, no "parity" to use a modern term, because all rights are conditioned on possibilities. If profits are very low then some inefficiency is involved or the product is not highly valued by society. There is also no upper limit on profits, but the businessman should share his profits in a spirit of equity.[8] It is important for the wealthy to voluntarily redistribute their wealth in accord with biblical norms. One might call this "charity" Ryan suggests, but it is obligatory nonetheless.

Ryan's working canons for distributive justice in wages are equality, need, effort and sacrifices, productivity, relative scarcity (supply and demand), and human welfare. In *A Living Wage,*[9] Ryan discusses at length the right to a living wage on the grounds of a worker's personal dignity and right to a decent livelihood under the conditions of modern industrialization in which wages represent the primary source of income for most people. Ryan gave the living wage underpinnings that address the modern situation. The human person is an end in her/himself and has a teleological orientation in which (s)he must live a life according to right reason. The highest goal of such a life is to know and to love God. The right to a living wage is thus based on this final end and exists as a means to promote the final end by supplying the individual with at least the minimum necessary goods. "Natural rights are necessary means of right and reasonable living."[10] Surpluses over the minimum necessary to meet the needs associated with human dignity may be distributed according to the other five canons.

Recognizing, I am sure, the very same realities brought out here in chapter 1, Ryan indicates that the strongest argument in favor of the market is economic efficiency. This efficiency, along with economic growth, receives strong support from the moral point of view in light of its contribution to meeting human needs and protecting human dignity. In this light, the payment of interest, profits, and rent to the suppliers of capital, entrepreneurial ability, and land respectively, are morally acceptable but inferior to labor's right to a living wage. I accept these findings.

As I mentioned earlier, in the strategy of the "redistributionist state," Ryan found a basic harmony between maximizing the general economic welfare and the demands of his ethics. Ryan's work gave support to three broad agenda items advanced in and after the days of the New Deal:

1. The state must manage the economy (through the use of expansionary fiscal and monetary policies) to raise the overall level of economic activity and especially employment.
2. The state may pursue other direct employment programs to increase employment.
3. For those who are employed, the state may pursue legislation to supplement labor income in various ways (such as the minimum wage law).

In this context, economic growth and supplementing labor income appear to be complementary goals.

American experience with these three is the subject of much of this chapter. Today, there is no longer the same optimism that expert government management can maintain the economy at full employment over the course of the business cycle, or effectively redistribute social benefits on the scale necessary to achieve economic justice. Second, there are related moral questions about the role of the state in human affairs, especially when viewed against the principle of subsidiarity. Third, new insight has been gained in recent years by the magisterium and some theologians in identifying the real moral significance of democratic capitalist systems. This new insight may be identified as a form of Christian Personalism which centers on the creative potential of human subjects who act in communities with others as the key to understanding the system from a moral viewpoint. Any remedy for our economic ills must incorporate this moral insight. Let us review American economic experience in the above three areas to see why this "first synthesis" is no longer an adequate synthesis between Catholic Social Thought and American economic practice.

High Hopes, Awful Outcomes: An Overview

The expert's (social scientist's) claim to status and reward is fatally undermined when we recognize that he possesses no sound stock of law-like generalizations and when we realize how weak the predictive power available to him is. . . . Our social order is in a very literal sense out of our, and indeed anyone's, control. No one is or could be in charge.[11]

Agenda Item One: Raising the Level of Economic Activity

In the 1960s it was believed that primarily through higher spending, and secondarily through a looser monetary policy, the government could successfully raise total spending which is the key to higher output and employment. This achieves the moral goal of assisting families and simultaneously helps to achieve economic growth. These were the prescriptions of Keynesian economics.[12] Through the mid 1960s, its adherents steadily grew in their confidence that the economy could be fine tuned through expert economic management.

However, it is not a proposition of Keynesianism today (and most certainly not a proposition of the more conservative supply side, monetarist, and rational expectations schools) that through monetary and fiscal policies unemployment can be reduced to and stabilized at the levels which might be morally acceptable.[13] This is true for two reasons. Present estimates of the full employment unemployment rate remain higher than what is considered morally acceptable, and the reality of the business cycle (successive periods of expansion and contraction in the level of business activity) makes stabilizing the rates at any level an ongoing problem.

Moral leaders in this country have lamented the acceptance of generally rising levels of unemployment (see table 2.1). Prior to the 1970s an unemployment rate of approximately 4 percent was thought to be an achievable full employment goal. This was the "full employment unemployment rate." Economists assume that there will always be some unemployment because there will always be unemployment from those entering the labor market for the first time and from those who voluntarily switch employers. However, given important structural changes in the contemporary labor market during the decades of the 1970s and 1980s, 6 to 7 percent unemployment was taken as the stable full employment unemployment rate which is attainable through expansionary policy. In recent years the labor market has come to include more teenagers, women, and other groups that tradi-

Table 2.1   *Statistical Abstract of the United States, 1997*
Employment Status of the Population

Year	Unemployed in Thousands	Percent of the Labor Force	Year	Unemployed in Thousands	Percent of the Labor Force
1970	4,093	4.9%	1995	7,404	5.6%
1980	7,637	7.1%	1996	7,236	5.4%
1985	8,312	7.2%	June 1998	6,237	4.5%
1990	7,047	5.6%			

Source: U.S. Bureau of the Census, *Statistical Abstract of the United States: 1997*, Washington, D.C. Table no. 621. Statistics for June 1998 come from the Bureau of Labor Statistics, *Employment Situation News Release*, table A–1. "Employment status of the civilian population by sex and age," July 1, 1998.

tionally have higher unemployment rates. In addition, government programs and the social welfare systems, broadly understood, lessen the hardship of unemployment. Consequently, there have also been other government attempts (programs) at job creation which do move beyond reliance on fiscal and monetary policy. Furthermore, continued supplementation of labor income would likely remain necessary even under the assumption of full employment given the presence of some very low-wage jobs. Very recent economic experience has again complicated the task of identifying the full employment unemployment rate. The current (as of 1998) economic expansion may suggest a full employment unemployment rate of approximately 4 to 5 percent.

Precisely because it is generally recognized today that the state cannot fully and reliably achieve, much less maintain, the desired end in this way, there have been other means pursued as well.

Agenda Item Two: Programs to Lower Unemployment

The more significant modern programs[14] dealing directly with employment and training began with the Manpower Development and Training Act (MDTA, first authorized in 1962), which was succeeded by the Comprehensive Employment and Training Act (CETA, 1973). CETA has itself been replaced by the present day Job Training Partnership Act (JTPA, 1983).

The MDTA addressed the problem of skilled workers who became structurally unemployed due to automation and technical change. The MDTA addressed the problem by providing retraining, relocation, and job information services. Later it became clear that this perception of the unemployment problem neglected the problem of unskilled workers, and the emphasis changed to include job training for lower income persons without job skills. This new emphasis on the unskilled workers was broadened to give additional benefit to unemployed young persons in the Economic Opportunity Act (EOA). The Emergency Employment Act (EEA) was passed in 1971 which was in the midst of an economic recession. This was the first major attempt at actual job creation since the New Deal. This act represented a new emphasis on job creation (instead of retraining) and local (not federal) control.

Comprehensive Employment and Training Act

The Comprehensive Employment and Training Act (CETA), constituted the most serious attempt to aid the unemployed with training and employment opportunities. CETA contains many parts and has had a very complex life before its termination in 1983 under President Reagan. As of 1973 CETA brought the MDTA, EOA, and EEA programs under one roof, but with significant changes.

The major issues in the drafting of CETA legislation concerned decentralization, decategorization, and public service employment.[15] President Nixon favored giving states more responsibility in decision making, planning, and administration of the program (decentralization). Nixon also favored allowing funds to be shifted among various alternative programs within CETA in accordance with the needs at the local level (decategorization). While Nixon favored expenditures for job training, he strongly opposed federally funded jobs which offered work to unemployed persons at the trough of the business cycle (public service employment). But with political realities being what they were, with a heavily Democratic Congress, and with rising unemployment at election time, Nixon was unable to stop the public service employment component of CETA which was to become a major characteristic of the program over time. Consistent with President Nixon's (Republican) emphasis on state's rights, CETA was characterized by decentralization, and decategorization (especially Title I), but it was also characterized by increased public service employment (Title II). The major components of CETA as first passed are show in table 2.2.

CETA continued to evolve until its end in 1983. With the recession and the resulting increased unemployment beginning in 1973, more emphasis was placed on public service employment and less on services to the unemployed. Programs under Title I were gradually replaced by Title II. Furthermore, combating the national recession tended to shift the emphasis in the program away from the economically disadvantaged and unskilled to offering jobs to all the unemployed.

CETA was reauthorized in 1978. By imposing stricter eligibility requirements, the reauthorization renewed the emphasis of the original act which was to help economically disadvantaged groups. Public service employment opportunities, which had been the principal cause of the growth in the cost of the program, were also cut back in the reauthorization.

Although CETA constituted the most significant attempt to aid the unemployed, the program was racked with criticism. There was the criticism of a "substitution effect" (that many CETA workers would have been hired by local entities even without the program). In other words, instead of taking on new workers, governments simply used the funds to pay regular employees. Based on various studies, estimates of this substitution effect ranged from 25 percent to as high as

Table 2.2   *The Major Components of CETA*

CETA Title	Provisions
I	Establishes a program of financial assistance to state and local governments (prime sponsors) for comprehensive personpower services. The sponsor determine the mix of design of services.
II	Allocates funds to hire unemployed persons in public service jobs.
III	Provides for federal supervision of the various programs.
IV	Incorporates and continues the Job Corps from the EOA under CETA legislation.
V	Establishes a National Manpower Commission.
VI	Contains provisions which apply to the entire legislation such as prohibitions against political activity and discrimination.

Source: Grace A. Franklin and Randall B. Ripley, CETA Politics and Policy (Knoxville: University of Tennessee Press, 1984), p.18.

60 percent after one year and from 40 percent to as high as 90 or 100 percent after two years.[16] It was not unusual for persons with masters degrees to be employed with CETA funds. Bad management and fraud charges also surfaced. Also interesting for our purposes is that even at its peak only 725,000 public service jobs were authorized by CETA under President Carter while the unemployment rate stood at 6.1 percent in 1978, or about 6.2 million people (excluding discouraged workers and the part-time underemployed). Therefore at its peak, CETA offered employment opportunities only to a very small percentage of the national unemployed.

The life of CETA ended in 1983 under President Reagan. CETA had suffered the slings and arrows of various criticisms, especially with respect to public service employment, and the program could not survive the conservative political tide which brought President Reagan to office. Economist George Johnson finds that while these programs can work to help those who need them, it is almost impossible actually to implement them within our present political system.[17] It is politically difficult to enact legislation that benefits only the least advantaged without provisions that benefit other groups. Even when programs to combat national problems are decentralized and decategorized, local and special interests have subverted the programs so that less needy groups benefit more, the substitution effect occurs, and other problems materialize.

Job Training Partnership Act

Over time CETA had acquired a horrible reputation. The successor to CETA is the Jobs Training Partnership Act (JTPA) of 1983. The act is well known today since sponsorship of the bill constituted a key item in the resume of Vice President Quayle. A *Congressional Quarterly* study in 1985 declared that "By wiping the slate clean . . . changing the law's name and modifying its governance structure—JTPA provided a new lease on life for federal job training strategies." The act expresses an increasing conservative/Republican commitment to decentralized and decategorized training programs for the most needy that work in cooperation with the private sector and are more closely monitored for cost effectiveness.

JTPA restores the older emphasis on job training while rejecting the emphasis on public service employment which had become such a large part of CETA under President Carter. No funds were provided for public service employment while 70 percent of funds were allocated explicitly for training. Funds did remain for wages paid by employers while workers receive on-the-job training, and some criticism of even this sort of wage payment emerged. It has been claimed that this really amounts to corporate welfare since workers in training are compensated in part by the program instead of by employers when employers have every reason to train their workers anyway.

The state governor, not the federal government, was made responsible for overall program coordination (decentralization). Local projects receive final approval at the state level, while under CETA principal oversight was exercised by the federal government. Local program management was entrusted to local Private Industry Councils (PICs). PICs are made up of 25 members on average and more than half are representatives from the business community. The PICs are free to establish job-training programs which they determine will best meet the needs of the local job market situation (decategorization). Under CETA local elected officials with local political jurisdiction managed the program.

The eligibility standards for JTPA are very similar to those for CETA. The low income and long-term unemployed are the targeted groups in both cases. However, a significant issue has emerged here. The use of performance standards and the participation of the business community in JTPA presents problems as well as advantages. Because JTPA gives greater voice to the business community in project design and management and because funds exist to serve only 4 percent of the eligible population, the fear has emerged that the needs of the least advantaged might not be well served. The concern is that the best available applicants will be skimmed off for assistance and training for more highly skilled positions without addressing the needs of those who are more needy and provide less return on investment. Indeed, early evaluations have found that ". . . in those SDA's (service delivery areas) without well defined client or service goals . . . performance standards can produce unintended effects of reducing service to the hard to serve and decreasing the intensity of services."[18]

Public attitude toward the program seems to be headed in the same direction as was the case with CETA. The new policy approaches adopted by the JTPA have been said to be a product of "images, myths, and idealogies"[19] held by CETA's prime opponents. JTPA has also been called the latest in an "alphabet soup of failed job programs,"[20] "Son of CETA,"[21] and "Quayle's Egg."[22] JTPA is receiving the same criticisms that relate to efficiency which buried its predecessor. For example, although Vice President Quayle could brag about the 68 percent national job placement rate for the program, Quayle did not mention that this national placement rate refers only to "graduates" and requires in most cases only one day on the job.[23] In one area (Tidewater, Virginia) 78 percent of those placed through the program terminated or were terminated within just six months. The program may not be serving the most needy, and may constitute a form of corporate welfare. Given the fantastic sums being spent and the ambiguous results, it seems difficult to be very sanguine about relying primarily on these public-sector activities to achieve economic justice.

Symbolic Actions

Elements within the U.S. government have attempted to commit the nation to full employment, but with little success. Like the Full Employment Act of 1945, The Humphrey-Hawkins Full Employment Act, finally passed in 1978, committed the United States to the goal of full employment in a purely symbolic way.[24] The evolution of this act shows that there are strong forces within the U.S. government that will not allow the unemployment problem to be attacked if such an attempt seems to contradict the goal of noninflation[25] or to be inordinately expensive.

The first version of the bill, H.R. 50, as drafted in 1974 was quite ambitious in the pursuit of full employment. It was sponsored by Augustus Hawkins (D) in the House and later by Hubert Humphrey (D) in the Senate. The early version aimed at full employment within five years and would have guaranteed all Americans over the age of sixteen, including the disadvantaged and the handicapped, a right to a job. This guarantee would have been worth something; the right to employment would have been enforceable through newly established administrative channels.

But then in 1975, a recession year, the bill was revised in several ways, perhaps the most important of which was the inclusion of price stability as a goal in this bill to counter the full employment emphasis.

A specific goal of 3 percent unemployment was also specified in this version as an interim goal. The third version represented a serious downward revision of the goals of the bill. Most importantly, the right to sue for a job was removed, and workers with special handicaps were no longer covered. Three percent unemployment was reaffirmed in this version but as a final goal. Yet this did not assure easy passage in the face of criticism from conservatives in business and government. Finally, the fourth version appeared and it represented the least aggressive version in combating unemployment. Four percent was established as an interim goal for unemployment, and inflation was to be reduced to 3 percent by 1983 and to zero by 1988. There were no mechanisms to force compliance with these goals, and full employment barely escaped as a priority over price stability. The high employment goals were clearly violated with impunity in subsequent years. The final law was clearly symbolic.

So there have been many programs to help the unemployed, and they have all been small relative to the problem which they were addressing. The acts that have truly aimed at full employment have been symbolic. At its peak only 725,000 public service jobs were authorized by CETA in 1978 while there were at least 6.2 million people without work.

Furthermore, these programs have been plagued by charges of various sorts of inefficiency. The programs have been dubbed "expensive" and the persons who are supposed to be helped by the programs have received inadequate benefit. It is also true that these programs have developed a bad reputation in the media, and political support for such programs is not strong.

We may summarize this discussion with the following conclusions:

1. There have been many programs to stabilize and maintain employment levels at full employment.
2. There has been a consistent movement in public policy toward decentralization, decategorization, and a movement away from direct government employment of the jobless.
3. Although expensive, state programs have all been inadequate relative to the problem that they were addressing.
4. It is very unlikely that political and public support can be maintained for even such limited programs that help the least advantaged.

　　5. The acts that have truly aimed at full employment have been symbolic.

Since we cannot promise employment at a living wage to all in the labor force, the need remains to deliver a living income. This brings us to the third public-sector strategy to bring about a more just distribution of income.

Agenda Item Three: Cash and In-Kind Transfers

The public sector does directly redistribute income and therefore wealth. The public sector has sought to supplement family income through a variety of programs. Stable full employment has been an elusive goal making the multiplication of assistance and social insurance programs an important strategy.

　　As is evident from table 2.3, social welfare expenditures under public programs have grown at a fantastic pace since the 1960s. These programs, rather than minimum wage laws, have been the focus for

Table 2.3　Social Welfare Expenditures under Public Programs in Per Capita (constant 1991 dollars)

	1960	1970	1980	1990	1991	1993
Social insurance	$ 460	$ 882	$1,662	$2,105	$2,196	$2,395
Public aid	97	267	528	600	705	809
Health and medical programs	107	156	198	262	271	272
Veterans' programs	132	145	155	125	126	131
Education	422	823	879	1,062	1,083	1,213
Housing	7	10	50	80	84	72
Other social welfare	27	67	99	74	77	83
Social welfare outlays in 1991 dollars, per capita TOTAL:	$1,252	$2,350	$3,571	$4,308	$4,542	$4,975

Source: U.S. Bureau of the Census, Statistical Abstract of the United States: 1991 Washington, D.C., Table no. 582; U.S. Bureau of the Census, Statistical Abstract of the United States: 1994 Washington, D.C., Table no. 572; and U.S. Bureau of the Census, Statistical Abstract of the United States: 1994 Washington, D.C., Table no. 576.

serious income redistribution. Money spent at federal, state, and local levels for social insurance, public aid, health and medical programs, veterans' programs, and public housing have increased dramatically over time on a per capita basis, taking inflation fully into account.

A more detailed breakdown of these seven major social welfare expenditure categories for 1991 is given in table 2.4. The data are for total outlays in millions of current dollars.

It is certainly true that considerable enthusiasm surrounded these programs in their beginnings. The "New Frontier," the "Great Society," the "War on Poverty," and other broad efforts raised expectations about the possibilities for achieving economic justice understood especially as the elimination or near elimination of poverty in the United States. Given the vast size of the expenditures and the persistence of extreme need, the results have been disappointing. Indeed, the programs expanded *most* rapidly during the decade of the 1970s. During that decade, social welfare expenditures under public programs increased a remarkable 52 percent while the poverty rate actually increased from 10.1 percent to 10.3 percent (table 2.5).

The programs have been dubbed "expensive" and it is commonly believed that persons who are supposed to be helped by the programs have received inadequate benefit. These programs have been plagued by charges related to two sorts of inefficiency. First, large sums of money are expended in the various administrative bureaucracies. Second, benefit from these programs is not entirely means tested; therefore, benefits are received by the nonpoor as well as the poor. This was an important problem under CETA and JTPA as well. Thomas Sowell has reported the following:[26]

> The amount necessary to lift every man, woman, and child in America above the poverty line has been calculated, and it is one-third of what is in fact spent on poverty programs. Clearly, much of the transfer ends up in the pockets of highly paid administrators, consultants, and staff as well as higher income recipients of benefits from programs advertised as antipoverty efforts.

Sowell's statement is dramatic and clearly over simplified; government provides services (and not only income) for a number of reasons. Nevertheless, his statements compel one to investigate, even if just to

Table 2.4   *Social Welfare Expenditures, by Source of Funds and Public Program, 1991*

Program	Federal	State and Local
Total	$ 676,406	$ 488,740
Social insurance	453,538	110,548
Old-age, survivors, disability, health	382,290	—
Health insurance (Medicare)	116,651	—
Public employee retirement	56,884	40,391
Railroad employee retirement	7,532	—
Unemployment insurance and employment services	3,613	27,700
Other railroad employee insurance	94	—
State temporary disability insurance	—	3,879
Workers' compensation	3,125	38,578
Hospital and medical benefits	506	15,503
Public aid	113,235	67,176
Public assistance	69,315	63,426
Medical assistance payments	53,393	47,740
Social services	2,117	706
Supplemental security income	15,896	3,751
Food stamps	19,471	—
Other	8,553	—
Health and medical programs	29,713	39,652
Hospital and medical care	16,790	12,636
Civilian programs	4,139	12,636
Defense Department	12,651	—
Maternal and child health programs	522	1,454
Medical research	9,793	1,494
Medical facilities construction	—	1,625
Other	2,608	22,443
Veterans' programs	32,331	526
Pensions and compensation	16,284	—
Health and medical programs	13,222	—
Hospital and medical care	12,190	—
Hospital construction	776	—
Medical and prosthetic research	256	—
Education	570	—
Life insurance	1,039	—
Welfare and other	1,217	526

Table 2.4   (Continued)

Program	Federal	State and Local
Education	$ 19,062	$ 258,063
Elementary and secondary	12,018	203,819
Construction	39	12,324
Higher	5,339	54,243
Construction	31	3,950
Vocational and adult	1,314	—
Housing	18,696	2,826
Other social welfare	9,831	9,949
Vocational rehabilitation	1,751	485
Medical services and research	439	121
Institutional care	142	523
Child nutrition	6,098	1,869
Child welfare	274	na
Special CSA and ACTION programs	192	—
Welfare, not elsewhere classified	1,375	7,071

Source: U.S. Bureau of the Census, *Statistical Abstract of the United States: 1994* (114th edition.) Washington, D.C., 1993. Table no. 573.

check the overall magnitude of the numbers. We can perform our own (admittedly rough) calculations for the year 1991. Expenditures at state and national levels for social insurance and public aid in 1991 were $744,497,000,000. We know that in 1991 a total of 7,712,000 families lived in poverty. Had the entire amount been given directly to families in poverty (a political and administrative impossibility) the division would yield $96,537 per family in poverty. The moral im-

Table 2.5   *Families below Poverty Level*

Year	Number in Thousands	Percent	Year	Number in Thousands	Percent
1960	8,243	18.1%	1985	7,223	11.4%
1970	5,260	10.1%	1990	7,098	10.7%
1980	6,217	10.3%	1995	7,532	10.8%

Source: U.S. Bureau of the Census, *Statistical Abstract of the United States: 1994* (114th edition.) Washington, D.C., Table no. 735.

peratives remaining here are that the growth of the administrative bureaucracies be checked and that benefits be distributed more closely according to need.

The late economist Arthur Okun,[27] former chairman of the Council of Economic Advisers under Democratic administrations, has written at length about this issue of "inefficiencies" involved in meeting economic rights. His analysis is helpful to explain the point.

For Okun, "rights" frequently do infringe on efficiency (output maximization). To guarantee a certain standard of living based on human rights, for example, is to reduce incentive to produce. But society has rightly decided to keep the market at bay in this and many other ways. The real case for inequality lies with the issue of efficiency. If industries are publicly owned or if income is redistributed away from productive members toward less productive members, efficiency will be reduced and the reduction is subject to empirical measurement.

The most important way to approach this problem is through the tax-transfer system. Using the analogy of a leaky bucket, Okun describes the problem as follows: We are transferring income from the rich to the poor in a bucket that leaks. The sources of the leakage are administrative costs in the transfers, reduced work effort by the productive ones of the system because of higher taxes, reduced funds for investment (unless the government is responsible enough to run a budgetary surplus), and a disincentive to work on the part of the poor. Okun is clear that meeting human rights, and in that sense living in a more humane society, has a material cost.

Indeed, progress in the struggle to raise the neediest American families out of their situation has been slow indeed, and Americans have become keenly aware of this. Anyone familiar with the political landscape of the United States since the defeat of Democratic congressional candidates in November 1994 and the appearance of the "Contract with America" would likely not contest the point. Clearly, a more sober attitude is indicated today about the possibilities and limitations of the redistributive state.

As can be seen in table 2.5, after some initial success between 1960 and 1970, the poverty rate has been fairly steady. It should, however, be noted that the poverty index excludes in-kind benefits in its calculations. Although in terms of total public expenditures in-kind assistance is growing at a much faster pace than "cash" assistance, food stamps, health care, and subsidized housing are not taken into account in the index. Therefore, the figures tend to overstate the numbers of persons "in poverty." It has been estimated that this has resulted in an overstatement of the poverty rate of approximately 2.6 percent.[28] At the same time, we may say that the figures tend to understate the effectiveness of social welfare expenditures.

These summary statistics also do not point out the major group which has indeed benefited enormously from public spending. Poverty among the aged has declined rapidly. The most important public spending factor here has been increasingly large social security payments. As recently as 1970, 24.6 percent of those over 65 years lived in poverty. In 1992 the figure had fallen to 12.9 percent.

To conclude this section, strategies which we may associate with Keynes (economics) and Ryan (ethics) can no longer be seen as guaranteeing employment and/or a living family income to all Americans. We noted the sorry fact that while the programs expanded most rapidly during the decade of the 1970s, the poverty rate increased nonetheless. Political experience and economic evidence bring us today to a conclusion quite different from Ryan's. This experience as summarized by Okun indicates that the state cannot harmonize the demands of ethics and economics through these traditional means of fine tuning the economy. I conclude that structural change will be necessary to achieve the demanding goals set by a moral perspective. I will make a constructive statement on this in chapter 5. For now, it is sufficient to note that simply to repeat Ryan's solution would show little understanding about the experienced limits of expansionary policy and of government programs.

The Enabling State

More recently, public-sector efforts have entered into a fourth strategy. The developments are recent, but I do want to briefly review what some economists say is happening and illustrate with emerging patterns in three major areas.

The public sector now seeks to harness the market in more subtle and more efficiently managed ways. There has been a growing recognition of precisely what has been documented here: public-sector efforts to provide all persons directly with employment or with a

Table 2.6   *Private Expenditures for Social Welfare*
             (in millions except for percent)

TYPE	1980	1985	1990	1991
Total Expenditures	$251,612	$456,288	$702,179	$756,365
Percent of GDP	9.3%	11.3%	12.9%	13.4%
Health	145,000	248,000	390,000	421,800
Income maintenance	51,169	116,207	160,876	171,016
Education	32,667	53,167	85,974	92,095
Welfare and other	22,776	38,914	65,329	71,454

Source: U.S. Bureau of the Census, *Statistical Abstract of the United States: 1994* (114th edition.) Washington, D.C., 1993. Table no. 575.

living income through cash and in-kind transfers have been costly and of disappointing effectiveness. Consequently, in what has come to be called a strategy of "the Enabling State,"[29] the public sector attempts to harness the private sector to achieve ends which it, with its battery of experts, determines. This is part of a larger movement in the direction of the market which began when JTPA significantly reduced the government's role in directly creating jobs (which had been a characteristic of CETA). Responsibility is pushed down, yet methods and ends are defined from above by experts and social planners.

Table 2.6 gives a statistical macroeconomic picture of the recent trend toward the growing contribution of the private sector for social welfare. I will briefly review examples of this evolving trend in the areas of health care, provisions for income maintenance in retirement, and public education.

Health Care

Approximately 11 percent of the total U.S. gross national product (GNP) is spent on health care. This is a staggering amount of money, especially when one considers that many of our poor in this country still lack access to adequate health care. Nevertheless, the fact that a majority within Congress and many sectors of the American public shied away from the health care planning of the Clinton administration is quite comprehensible. It seems that a successful health care reform will likely include greater emphasis on privatization, individual responsibility, the use of incentives, and decentralization as means to achieve better health care. This may better describe the direction of recent changes in the decade prior to the Clinton plan:

> On the finance side, public insurance for health care has moved in this direction through the introduction of market-oriented reimbursement mechanisms and efforts to increase private payments. . . .
>
> On the production side of health care provisions, the commercial orientation is powerfully impelled by the growth of corporate providers. . . . "Those who talked about 'health care planning' in the 1970s now talk about 'health care marketing.' "[30]

The appearance of Health Maintenance Organizations (HMOs) symbolizes the sort of health care reform in the private sector that has recently gained much ground. Through managed care and administrative oversight, HMOs look to control costs. HMOs were pioneered in the 1940s by Kaiser-Permanente,[31] which operates and continues to expand in a number of states. Nurses have also figured highly in the recent industrywide shifts. Some 35,000[32] nurses have now entered into private practice in various capacities by opening their own businesses and providing cost-effective care. Furthermore, the 1980s saw experiments with health care vouchers and price setting for Medicaid and Medicare patients.[33]

The appearance of HMOs has of course not been without controversy. There is a growing perception that HMOs provide good cost management, but there are questions about the quality of services that they provide. There have thus been calls for increasing regulation of HMOs to protect the quality of patient care. Sixty percent of Americans do support "tougher government regulation of managed care programs like HMO's," but this falls to a meager 37 percent if that legislation were to raise costs.[34] This desire for regulation does not, therefore, constitute a rejection of the broad philosophy of HMOs, but only a desire to optimize the system to ensure and protect patient care.

In the future I would not look for the sort of centralized health care management for which the early Clinton administration became known; we might look rather for the state to harness the energies of the health care market while showing due respect for privatization, individual responsibility, the use of incentives, and decentralization in the pursuit of affordable and quality health care.

Income Maintenance and Reform Initiatives

We have also seen greater reliance on individual responsibility, the use of incentives, and decentralization integrated into the various income maintenance programs which are financed primarily by the federal government:

> Indirect expenditures that subsidize private pensions for the elderly, workfare reforms to promote employment of AFDC mothers, and refundable tax credits in support of the working poor are three arrangements that have gained an increasing role in income maintenance since the 1960's. Each of these cases lend favor to private enterprise and the work ethic. In so doing, these welfare transfers forge a link between social and economic markets that contributes to the emerging structure of modern welfare capitalism.[35]

Modest but philosophically significant attempts were made in the early 1980s to shift the burden of caring for the elderly away from the public sector and reliance on social security. The Reagan administration with its promotion of Individual Retirement Accounts (IRAs) offered means and incentive to save for one's own retirement. Workers were allowed to contribute up to an annual maximum of $2,000 to a tax-deferred retirement account. The money would be available at retirement when one's income and tax rate are both presumably lower. Furthermore, in 1981 the tax-exempt amount for private KEOGH plans was doubled. Such measures, combined with a growth in private pensions, have shifted much of the responsibility for maintaining the income of seniors back into the private sector.

Aid to Families With Dependent Children (AFDC) is one excellent example of a program that historically has come in for remarkable criticism on the basis of inequities, inefficiencies, disincentives to work, the promotion of out-of-wedlock births, and the creation of a long-term dependency among a hard core of recipients. The program is state administered but with significant federal funding. AFDC offers support to families who lack financial support because of a parental death, disability, divorce, or desertion.

The disintegration of the family structure and the large number of children in poverty are among the most salient features in any contemporary analysis of AFDC. Increasingly we see a greater number of females who alone bear the financial (and other) burden(s) of heading a family and a stunning number of children living in poverty. In 1991 21.1 percent[36] of all children lived in poverty. This does not surprise since the poverty line is defined according to family size and income, and the simple birth of a child can statistically drive a family into poverty. This is such a significant factor that children are sometimes listed among the "causes"[37] of poverty. Indeed, it is speculated that the availability of benefits not only helps to alleviate the problem of poverty but also contributes to it by influencing behavior in childbearing years.

Because the program is state administered, there have been a variety of attempts to reform it. In the 1980s California and Massachusetts AFDC recipients were offered services that could include job training, child care, and employment assistance and were subject to a work-for-benefits requirement. Although these reforms and requirements have not generated particularly strong results, there was broad-based recognition that significant reform was an urgent need. In August 1996 President Clinton signed into law the "Personal Responsibility and Work Opportunity Reconciliation Act," the new welfare reform law that established the "Temporary Assistance for Needy Families" (TANF) program. This legislation is more decentralized than AFDC, its predecessor. Furthermore, the states have dramatically increased flexibility to design welfare programs to meet the particular needs of welfare families. Given the creation by AFDC of a long-term dependency among a hard core of recipients, the federal government now demands measurable results related to moving families into self-sufficiency. This reform, heavily influenced by Republican majorities in Congress, represents a continuation, perhaps radicalization, of the philosophical development reviewed here in the nation's welfare system. Decentralization and decategorization are strongly evident, as is a bolder commitment to employment for the needy in the private sector.

The legislation provides for tough work requirements, bonuses to reward states for moving welfare recipients into jobs, uncompromising child support enforcement, increased funding for child care and medical coverage, and other supports for moving families from welfare into work in the private sector. Factsheets released by the Department of Health and Human Services (August 12, 1997), claimed that the welfare caseload fell by 3.4 million recipients from 14.1 million recipients in January 1993 to 10.7 million in May 1997, a drop of 24 percent since 1992 and representing the lowest percentage of the population on welfare since 1970. According to the Council of Economic Advisors (CEA) analysis, over 40 percent of the reduction in the welfare rolls can be attributed to the very strong economic growth during recent years, nearly one-third can be attributed to waivers granted to states to test innovative strategies to move people from welfare to work, and the rest is attributed to other factors, which are speculated to include the expansion of the Earned Income Tax Credit, strengthened child support enforcement, and increased funding for child care.

Decentralization, decategorization, and a bold commitment to employment for the needy in the private sector have seemingly produced some remarkable empirical results. However, I believe that we cannot know at this point ultimately how well these particular reforms will succeed and just how they must be modified in the future. The reforms are in many ways still in their infancy, and a number of honest and hard questions must be asked. What is the relationship between the recent increase in human abortions in some states and the reduction in welfare benefits for second children? What is the relationship between the number of persons no longer receiving welfare and the number of homeless in this country? How well can these reforms really protect the dignity of the mentally ill who may be unemployable? Although I take decentralization, decategorization, and the commitment to employment for the needy in the private sector as three key aspects of U.S. moral experience and illustrative of the principle of "subsidiarity," we must remain nondogmatic about, and carefully alert to, the actual long-run consequences of any particular programs. Commitment to social justice is never simply to be equated with commitment to any particular program.

The *overriding* goal is to move persons off public assistance and into self-sufficiency through productive employment in private-sector jobs. Therefore, there can hardly be a higher moral priority than creating an environment in the private sector in which persons can find jobs that are both personally satisfying and enable them to meet their material needs. Subsequent chapters in this book will lay out the moral and economic argument for the creation of precisely such an important environment.

Education

Education spending for public education in the United States also raises questions about spending, taxes, public-sector effectiveness, and the proper role of the federal government with which we may finalize the argument here. In 1979 the U.S. Department of Education (DOE), previously the Office of Education, became a cabinet-level agency. Since that time, the role of the federal government in public education in the fifty states has increased steadily. Unfortunately, the results have driven many students out of the government schools and into private education.

Between 1972 and 1994, scores for the scholastic aptitude test (SAT) have fallen by thirty-five points.[38] Over this same period, per-student expenditures in constant dollars within public education rose a remarkable 48.5 percent.[39] 1994 annual expenditures per students in the United States were $5,314.

In New York, my own state of residence, national problems in education have reached the point that they are absolutely impossible to overlook from either an academic or moral perspective. John Taylor Gatto, New York State Teacher of the Year, has written the following:

> The one point that elected officials, bureaucrats, administration, and teachers unions agree on is that somehow, despite the fact that taxes and education expenditures continue to rise unabated in New York, we are shortchanging our children and their education by not paying enough. The median private school tuition in the United States is slightly under $3,000; the median parochial school tuition is about $2,300. Yet in New York State, where public school per-seat expenditures exceed $9,000 per year, it has been determined that $9,000 is not enough.

Educational quality has decayed in New York while real per pupil expenditures have risen dramatically. While we recognize the limitations of standardized tests as measures of quality, on virtually any criterion we can name, the general perception of citizens, churches, institutions, journalists, et al. is that we are producing an intellectual and moral catastrophe.[40]

Gatto has suggested that the state resort to voucher plans by which parents would be enabled to send their children to schools of their choosing as a way of lowering costs and creating the competition which might raise educational quality. However, the New York State teachers union has resisted vigorously and successfully. Indeed, in 1992 the New York State United Teachers union contributed more money to legislative races than any other political action committee in the state.[41] New York is hardly alone in such experiences with the public education establishment.

The nation's capital is home to what may be the most ineffective school system in the United States, which impairs both the economic future of those students as well as the economic future of the society in which they are members. These students are trapped in a cycle of poverty and failure, and the existing public education system is part of that entrapment. Although school choice programs have been shown to narrow the gap in test scores between whites and minorities by 33 percent to 50 percent in the school choice experiments in Milwaukee, Wisconsin and Cleveland, Ohio,[42] Republican efforts (with some bipartisan support) to bring about school choice in the capital have been resisted by the public education establishment. Indeed, on May 20, 1998 President Clinton did veto such a bill. The "D.C. Student Opportunity Scholarship Act of 1997" would have provided scholarships of up to $3,200 to approximately 1,800 *poor* children in grades K–12. An important opportunity to attack the cycle of poverty and raise the fortunes economically and otherwise for a significant number of children was missed.

Again, in the public sector we find that colossal levels of spending have failed to bring about the intended results. Education is experiencing increasing centralization, rising costs, and falling performance. As remedy, the DOE, with strong support from the National Education Association, has proposed further increased spending and centralization.

The DOE supports "Goals 2000" legislation which redefines and expands the mission of public education while simultaneously increasing the role of the federal government in education. Public education will now address the needs of "all" learners. "All," in the context of Goals 2000 and accompanying legislation, includes children before entry into kindergarten,[43] children who do not attend government schools, and adults who today must become accustomed to "life long learning." The mission is further expanded to give more explicit and systematic attention to the social and emotional behaviors of children.

In cooperation with the Department of Labor, perhaps *the* most important mission redefinition is to make a "School-to-Work Opportunities System" out of public education. J.D. Hoye, director of the federal School-to-Work Opportunities Office for the U.S. DOE, cites falling U.S. productivity levels along with the need for higher practical skills in support of the mission redefinition.[44] This effort will redefine "learning outcomes" for each grade level to include skills necessary for vocational employment and will involve partnerships with business and labor groups in setting K–12 objectives. Although the DOE insists that compliance with the legislation is "voluntary," receipt of funds under the Elementary and Secondary Education Act (ESEA) is largely conditioned on compliance with the federal Goals 2000.

The legislation and its state-level correlates[45] have met with remarkable organized resistance by parents and some educators in the states of Colorado, Kansas, Minnesota, New Hampshire, Oklahoma, Pennsylvania, Washington, Ohio, Iowa, Wyoming, and Connecticut. Many states have rejected pieces of the reform effort, while a few have rejected the funds entirely because of the federal strings which have been attached.

Parental organizations in the different states tend to raise similar objections. Current education reform remodels education according to a vocational education model as it sets back the cause of "liberal education." Although these reforms are intended by education experts to help solve the problems of unemployment, inequality, and other social ills, they may do the reverse. Indeed, without a liberal education, we shall raise a generation that is even less able to ask the important questions about human life that are key to solving many social and ethical problems. Furthermore, parents of gifted students complain that it fails to meet the needs of their children. Perhaps the most successful such organization in the nation, "Connecticut Save Our Schools" (CT-SOS), has eighty chapters and is known for its ten-point reform plan. A cofounder of the organization, Kay Wall, was nominated to the state board of education. However, efforts by the Connecticut teachers unions denied her the votes in the legislature which would have been necessary to win confirmation. The Connecticut teachers unions pose an indissolubly linked combination of power and money which gave them the means to protect the status quo. Ms. Wall withdrew her nomination in April 1995. The ten-point plan may be summarized as follows:[46]

1. Reject federal interference. This point holds a preeminence over all other CT-SOS reform proposals.
2. Relieve teachers from certification. This allows the hiring of teachers trained outside the schools of education.
3. Inject the free market. Charter schools are encouraged.
4. Prune state mandates. Nonacademic state mandates have diminished local control and taken away from academics.
5. Enact a "Sunshine" provision. Public inspection of all state tests should be possible after two years.
6. Require standardized tests. Comparisons (between schools, districts, and states) must be made to improve education.
7. Provide for disruptive students. Students should be heterogeneously grouped as necessary, with special accommodations made for disruptive students.
8. Protect student privacy.
9. Reduce overhead.
10. Identify the reading curriculum. CT-SOS claims to favor a "phonics" approach over the "whole language" approach.

In many ways, these points bring to clarity the heart of the criticisms made about the government's attempts at social assistance. These well-intentioned attempts at social assistance by the state have raised serious doubts about cost, effectiveness, and emphasized the needs for private control and decentralization. On this set of issues the approach of the "enabling state" is healthy. Yet the approach still lacks attention to a second set of issues: the need for values and the identification of ends to flow upward, not downward in a tyrannical way. To take education as an example, the perspective of the enabling state should lead us to a system of school choice, but the accompanying danger will be the possibility of undue government influence on religious and private schools. This would endanger the most important contribution which these schools make to the students who attend: the imparting of character, values, and a distinctive worldview formed in continuity with some religious or other tradition. Analogously, in the case of health care, income maintenance, and education, the enabling state must attend to both sets of issues: local control *and* local values and conceptions about worldview. The success of government initiatives will depend in significant degree on the extent to which community-based organizations (CBO's), such as CT-SOS in this one example, are involved.

The Moral Objection

Recent years have seen a host of questions raised about what the proper role of the state should be in the lives of its citizens from the moral perspective. The practical bases for this concern have just been described. We must also ask the question: if these policies and programs pursued at the federal and state levels failed to achieve the desired results, can we also say a word about the moral reasons for their failure? Such reasons have already been powerfully identified by John Paul II and developed by Michael Novak.

John Ryan, with his essentially Keynesian perspective on economics, had stressed the role of the state in the solution to economic problems. However, there is concern that the programs based on this strategy do not show sufficient understanding about the human person that would be necessary to make them successful. On the bases of a Christian Personalist perspective, John Paul II emphasizes the role of moral responsibility which is most appropriately exercised by social groups and individuals:

> By intervening directly and depriving society of its responsibility, the Social Assistance State leads to a loss of human energies and an inordinate increase of public agencies, which are dominated more by

bureaucratic ways of thinking than by concern for serving their clients, and which are accompanied by an enormous increase in spending. In fact, it would appear that needs are best understood and satisfied by people who are closest to them and who act as neighbors to those in need. . . . [P]eople can be helped effectively only by those who offer them genuine fraternal support, in addition to the necessary care.[47]

Personalism recognizes those needs that persons have that can only be satisfied outside of the bureaucracies of the state. Persons must exercise what is their primary capital; they must exercise their own initiative and use their personal talents with the fraternal support of neighbors. The "social assistance state" is the more legitimate welfare state that has overextended itself in its direct assistance and underextended itself by failing to promote social life in its various forms, which include civic organizations, churches, schools, families, and other forms. These ideas are so important that they are summarized in a well-known principle of Catholic Social Thought: subsidiarity. This principle was given definition by Pope John XXIII in *Mater et Magistra:*

> It is a fundamental principle of social philosophy, fixed and unchangeable, that one should not withdraw from individuals and commit to the community what they can accomplish by their own enterprise and industry. So, too, it is an injustice and at the same time a grave evil and a disturbance of right order, to transfer to the larger and higher collectivity functions which can be performed and provided for by lesser and subordinate bodies.[48]

John Paul II offers a helpful statement especially where the moral dimensions of economic life are concerned:

> Whereas at one time the decisive factor of production was the land, and later capital—understood as a total complex of the instruments of production—today the decisive factor is increasingly man himself, that is, his knowledge, especially his scientific knowledge, his capacity for interrelated and compact organization, as well as his ability to perceive the needs of others and to satisfy them.[49]

John Paul points out what any Christian Personalism worthy of the name could hardly overlook. Of course, in all ages the moralist ought to pay careful attention to a proper understanding of the individual who exists only in communities with others. But the modern era has made it totally inexcusable to overlook this perspective. It is not tangible capital but the talent, knowledge, and skills which reside in women and men which are decisive for economic life today. Exercising these is the condition for the possibility of economic growth and the meeting of human rights.

Conclusion

The redistributive state has made some progress in achieving a more equitable distribution of income. Redistribution has occurred through attempts at increasing employment and more directly by cash and in-kind transfers. We have, for example, seen poverty rates fall dramatically for the aged. The redistributive approach in which Ryan shared has made a permanent contribution to social ethics. The quite urgent moral imperatives remaining here are that the growth of the administrative bureaucracies be checked and that benefits be distributed more closely according to need.

However, given the fantastic sums being spent and the ambiguous results, it seems difficult to be satisfied with the sort of statism which would look so heavily, almost exclusively, toward public-sector management to achieve economic justice. The true believers of this old-time religion will continue to insist that all we need is even tighter, more expert control of the economy; they will be aided and abetted by similarly minded religious persons. These will continue to support this old-time interventionist religion for a number of reasons: they take their economic ethics directly and without mediating concepts from the Scriptures which generally presume an agrarian and zero-sum economy; or they are at heart more influenced by the New Deal than by Christian principles; or they lack evidence. Yet, I do believe that the enthusiasm and energies for this approach are spent.

Perhaps it is best to look at direct government redistribution as a sort of triage which is appropriate in an immediate and short-run situation in which human welfare is endangered and cannot be protected in any other way. There will always be an important role for governments in the pursuit of justice. We must of course feed the hungry and cloth the naked *immediately*. But redistribution of this sort has shown itself not to be a sustainable method in the long run to meet human needs and to provide for human flourishing which must include the development of the productive capacities of the poor. A hospital that only performs triage is an absurdity.

Furthermore, even if a technical possibility, the moral objections made from a Christian Personalist perspective would still remain. Issues which have arisen relating to human agency, the relation between the state and society, individual incentive, social dependency, family and communal life, and human need to pursue value, indicate that progress on the question of economic justice (distributive and otherwise) can only be had through a new consideration of economic justice along with the anthropological question. The next two chapters bring contemporary liberal theory into dialogue with Catholic Social Thought to develop such a social anthropology and a Personalist perspective on economic justice.

In chapter 3 we examine the major works of important thinkers (Rawls, Nozick, Walzer) who mirror in a systematized way the experience with public policy reviewed here. This gives the needed theoretical clarity to the national experience recounted and explication to the "individualism - statism" dialectic. Furthermore, the Personalist anthropology developed in chapter 4 presupposes key elements of chapter 3 as it borrows from liberal theory which shows a great appreciation and grounding for liberty and equality. Christian Personalism can be grateful for a carefully measured dose of the liberal influence.

Notes

1. For the details of Father Ryan's biography, I rely on: Francis L. Broderick, *Right Reverend New Dealer: John A. Ryan* (New York: Macmillan Publishing Co., 1963).
2. Perhaps the most notable figures were Archbishop John Ireland of St. Paul in the liberal group and Archbishop Michael A. Corrigan of New York among the conservatives. In fact, it was Archbishop Ireland who ordained Ryan to the priesthood in 1898.

3. See: Charles Curran, *American Catholic Social Ethics* (Notre Dame, Indiana: University of Notre Dame Press, 1982), p.26.

4. Keynes first published his *General Theory of Employment, Interest, and Money* in 1936. It was this work that so revolutionized economic thinking, moving it beyond the classical model.

5. John Ryan, *Distributive Justice* (New York: Macmillan Publishing Co., 1942).

6. Ryan, *Distributive Justice*, p.96.

7. Ryan, *Distributive Justice*, p.343.

8. Longer range policy recommendations include vertical integration to eliminate middleman profits and increasing the number of people educated to become businessmen to increase the supply and thereby reduce individual profit shares. Profits by monopolies are unjust when they are the result of market power. The government should discourage monopoly and unjust monopoly practices.

   Ryan also suggests more immediate legislative remedies. A system of progressive income taxes could prevent the accumulation of great fortunes and reduce great fortunes in existence. A minimum wage law would bring great improvement in the situation of the poor and the nation by providing increased demand (a Keynesian argument). This would be an effective and also a moral solution. Workers may justly exploit the possible gains from unionization.

9. John Ryan, *A Living Wage: Its Ethical and Economic Aspects* (New York: Macmillan Publishing Co., 1912).

10. Ryan, *A Living Wage*, p.48.

11. Alasdair MacIntyre, *After Virtue* (Notre Dame, Indiana: University of Notre Dame Press, 1981), p.101.

12. I do not wish overly to expand the discussion here into the details of macroeconomic theory and its use in Christian ethics. Those interested may refer to: Richard C. Bayer, "Do We Want a Christian Economics? The U.S. Bishops' Pastoral Letter," *Theological Studies* 51(1990), pp.627–49.

13. The American Catholic bishops in *Economic Justice for All* indicate a morally satisfactory unemployment rate as being in the 3 to 4 percent range.

14. Programs to assist the unemployed did not first appear in the 1960s. The New Deal policies of President Franklin D. Roosevelt designed to combat the unemployment of the Great Contraction established many such programs—the largest of which were the Public Works Administration, the Civil Works Administration, the Works Progress Administration, the Civil Conservation Corps, the National Youth Administration, and the

Social Security Act. President Franklin D. Roosevelt is the father of government training and employment programs. However, unemployment remained high until 1941 when it averaged nearly 10 percent. Full employment was not reached until rising military spending and conscription lowered the unemployment rate to under 2 percent during World War II. Full employment was not reached through the New Deal programs. This reduction in the unemployment rate due to the war did not go unnoticed at the time, and the Full Employment Act of 1946 was enacted over widespread concern that the unemployment rate would rise after the war.

New Deal programs were mostly short-lived attempts to address the problem of the Great Contraction, and until the 1960s the federal government showed little tangible interest in the problem of unemployment with the exception of the partial funding of unemployment insurance. The recent round of federal programs to increase employment and supplement family income find their beginning in the 1960s.

15. Grace A. Franklin and Randall B. Ripley, *CETA Politics and Policy* (Knoxville: University of Tennessee Press, 1984), p.13.

16. Janet W. Johnston, "An Overview of U.S. Federal Employment and Training Programs," in *Unemployment, Policy Responses of Western Democracies,* ed. Jeremy Richardson and Roger Hennig (Beverly Hills, California: SAGE Publishing, 1984), p.71.

17. George E. Johnson, "Employment and Training Programs in the United States: What Do We Know, and Where Should We Go from Here?" in *The American Work Force: Labor and Employment in the 1980's,* ed. Robert A. Ullrich (Dover, Massachusetts: Auburn Press, 1984).

18. *JTPA Performance Standards, Executive Summary* (Washington D.C.: National Commission for Employment Policy, 1988), p.5.

19. Donald C. Baumer and Carl E. Van Horn, *The Politics of Unemployment* (Washington, D.C.: Congressional Quarterly Inc., 1985), p.179.

20. "The Failure of Federal Job Training Programs," *USA Today,* July 1987, p.13.

21. "Son of CETA," *The New Republic,* April 14, 1986, p.16.

22. "Quayle's Egg," *The New Republic,* September 12 & 19, 1988, p.19.

23. "The Failure of Federal Job Training Programs," *USA Today,* July 1987, p.16.

24. Helen Ginsburg, *Full Employment Policy: The United States and Sweden* (Lexington, Massachusetts: Lexington Books, 1983), ch. 3.

25. Economists believe the evils of inflation are many. Inflation makes business and economic planning difficult since costs and prices are not

easily predicted. Inflation tends to redistribute buying power from savers to debtors (especially if the inflation is unanticipated) and arbitrarily punishes those on a fixed income.

26. Thomas Sowell, *Markets and Minorities* (New York: Basic Books, Inc., 1981), p.122.

27. See: A.M. Okun, *Equality and Efficiency—the Big Tradeoff* (Washington, D.C.: Brookings Institution, 1975).
    Okun, "Further Thoughts on Equality and Efficiency," in J. Pechman (ed.), *Economics for Policymaking* (Cambridge, Massachusetts: MIT Press, 1983).

28. Sar Levitan, *Programs in Aid of the Poor* (Baltimore, Maryland: Johns Hopkins University Press, 1990), p.3.

29. Neil Gilbert and Barbara Gilbert, *The Enabling State* (New York: Oxford University Press, 1989).

30. Gilbert, *The Enabling State,* pp.135–6.

31. Gilbert, *The Enabling State,* p.130.

32. Gilbert, *The Enabling State,* p.136.

33. While these methods can provide incentives to reduce costs, the charge has been made that they also provide incentive to reduce the quality of care in order to maintain profit.

34. Statistical Source: Gary Langer, ABC NEWS Polling Analyst, *Support for HMO Regulation is Conditioned on the Cost,* ABCNEWS.com, July 15, 1998. Langer also notes that 80 percent of those actually enrolled in an HMO are satisfied with the quality of care.

35. Gilbert, *The Enabling State,* p.97.

36. U.S. Bureau of the Census, *Statistical Abstract of the United States: 1994* (114th edition.) Washington, D.C., 1993. Table no. 728. The percent of children below the poverty level by race in 1992 was: white 16.0 percent; black 46.3 percent; Hispanic 38.8 percent.

37. Levitan, *Programs in Aid of the Poor,* p.21.

38. The American Legislative Exchange Council, *Report Card on American Education 1994* (Washington, D.C.: Office of Public Affairs-Publications, 1994), p.16.

39. The American Legislative Exchange Council, *Report Card on American Education 1994,* p.22. Dollar figures were adjusted for inflation using 1994 constant dollars.

40. John Taylor Gatto and Raymond J. Keating, *The Accountability Myth: An Introduction to New York State Education Reform* (New York: New York Citizens for a Sound Economy Foundation, 1994), p.6.

41. Gatto, *The Accountability Myth,* p.11.

42. Nina H. Shokraii, *How Congress Can Help Poor Children Learn in D.C.*

Schools, The Heritage Foundation, Executive Memorandum no. 483, June 3, 1997.

43. Indeed, the first of the eight goals of Goals 2000 concerns the preparation of children *before* entry into the system. As stated by the DOE. The eight goals of Goals 2000 are:

    1. All children in America will start school ready to learn.
    2. The high school graduation rate will increase to at least 90 percent.
    3. All students will leave grades 4, 8, and 12 having demonstrated competency over challenging subject matter.
    4. The United States will be first in the world in mathematics and science achievement.
    5. Every adult American will be literate and will possess the knowledge and skills necessary to compete in a global economy and exercise the rights and responsibilities of citizenship.
    6. Every school in the United States will be free of drugs and violence.
    7. The nation's teaching force will have access to programs for the continued improvement of their professional skills.
    8. Every school will promote partnerships that will increase parental involvement and participation in promoting the social, emotional, and academic growth of children.

44. I take this from a specially televised address to New York educators on May 17, 1995 at a School-to-Work conference. Hoye had been scheduled to appear personally.

45. Individual states are enacting parallel pieces of reform legislation (or state education department directives) which holds them in compliance with the national efforts. In New York State the blueprint for education reform is the *New Compact for Learning.*

46. This is based on a list directly from CT-SOS at: *The Committee to Save Our Schools,* P.O. Box 5222, Westport, CT 06881, 454-SAVE (7283). The points also appeared in an opinion-editorial: Ken von Kohorn, Cofounder of CT-SOS, "Beware of Federal Interference in Our Public Schools," in the *Minuteman,* (Westport, Connecticut, October 6, 1994), p.18.

47. John Paul II, *Centesimus Annus,* par. 48.

48. John XXIII, *Mater et Magistra,* par. 53.

49. John Paul II, *Centesimus Annus,* par. 32.

II

CAPITALISM WITHOUT INDIVIDUALISM

3

The Liberal Anthropology:
Free, Equal, and Rational

And I ask the three of you, how can we, as symbolically the
children of the future president, expect . . . you to meet our
needs, the needs in housing and in crime and you name
it? — Audience Participant in 1992 Presidential Debate

Although work remains to be done, Michael Novak has done much
to show the historical connections and disconnections between the
traditions of philosophical liberalism and Catholic Social Thought.
Novak's call[1] to continue such a discussion between these two traditions is an important one. Our task is different and not historical, but
oriented more to what liberalism has become than to what theoretical
connections may have existed between the two traditions in the past.
The development of a contemporary Christian Personalist social ethic
requires us to examine contemporary works that offer us insight into
the strengths and problematics of liberalism *today*. Time has certainly
taken a toll in that liberalism today stands at greater distance from its
shared roots with Christian theology. This is especially the case when
we speak about the various notions of the human person, human
agency, and human community.

The stunning and infantile question (above) posed by an audience
participant in the presidential debate demonstrates the remarkable
extent to which many Americans seem to have placed their deepest
hopes and longings in the power of the state, and not in themselves
and in those associations closer to them, for a just society in which
citizens are enabled to lead the good life. Indeed, the press treated
the question as common sense incarnate in the process of dismissing

the "character question" as nearly irrelevant for a successful presidency (we have since learned better!). We turn to a contemporary discussion within American liberal philosophy in order really to grasp the understanding in its fullness of the human person and human agency which inform such a perspective. Keep in mind that it is precisely this dismal state of affairs to which the Personalist anthropology must address itself—incorporating insights and speaking prophetically.

I emphasize and begin with what is commonly believed to be the most significant works in American political philosophy this century. The three works in order of treatment are: *A Theory of Justice* by John Rawls, *Spheres of Justice* by Michael Walzer, and *Anarchy, State, and Utopia* by Robert Nozick. There is, to my mind, no better and more insightful discussion within contemporary liberalism about the nature of justice and its moral foundations than exists in these three works. Indeed, for Alasdair MacIntyre, Rawls and Nozick in particular have produced leading works in analytical moral philosophy which also give expression to the dominant popular perspectives in American politics today.[2] The useful and the problematic in the liberal anthropologies will be sorted out here as we pay attention to their criticisms of each other and to criticisms leveled from explicitly Christian perspectives.

The three theories of justice discussed here contain an understanding of the human person which is central to the entire theory. For reasons that will become apparent, a Christian Personalist cannot adopt in total any of the understandings of the human person contained in these theories of justice. But first, there is much to learn from this remarkable debate.

John Rawls

A Theory of Justice is a powerful, deep, subtle, wide ranging, systematic work in political and moral philosophy which has not seen its like since the writings of John Stuart Mill, if then. It is a fountain of illuminating ideas, integrated together into a lovely whole. Political philosophers now must either work within Rawls' theory or explain why not.[3]

In part one of *A Theory of Justice,* the primary subject of justice is explained in this way:[4]

> For us the primary subject of justice is the basic structure of society, or more exactly, the way in which the major social institutions distribute fundamental rights and duties and determine the division of advantages from social cooperation. By major institutions I understand the political constitution and the principal economic and social arrangements.

It is assumed that primary goods, which are goods that any self-interested person would want to advance her/his life plans, are distributed by social institutions and are seven in number:[5] rights, liberties, self-respect, power, opportunities, income, and wealth. Rawls calls this the "thin theory of the good" and offers no deeper justification for it.[6] The way in which the major social institutions function must be governed by the principles of justice. The principles agreed to are general, that is "it must be possible to formulate them without the use of what would be intuitively recognized as proper names, or rigged definite descriptions".[7] They must be universal in application. They must be public in that everyone will know about these principles. They must impose an order on conflicting claims, and they must be final. The choice of these principles is perhaps the heart of this theory.

The choice is made by persons in the hypothetical "original position" which parallels the state of nature of social contract theory. These persons are contemporaries of an unknown generation. The original position is given a complex specification. Parties in the original position are free, equal, rational, self-interested, and they are held behind a veil of ignorance. They do not know their place in society, they have no idea about how well they will fare in the natural lottery of talents, nor do they know their likes, dislikes, religious beliefs, etc. They know only the general facts about human society. It is assumed that they have different aims (life plans), but they cannot advance them at the cost of others since all knowledge is held behind the veil of ignorance. Ignorance of these things guarantees impartiality in the choice of principles and leads the parties to behave in a very risk-averse way in a choice of principles by which society is organized to distribute the primary goods. Also, without the veil all would pursue their self-interest and no agreement would be possible.

Furthermore, as Rawls was to make clear in his 1985 article in response to controversy, the original position is not to be interpreted metaphysically as offering us a full understanding about the nature of a human person. This was the interpretation put forth most prominently by Michael Sandel.[8] The original position is to be interpreted politically as an exercise by rational people in the hope of finding an "overlapping consensus" in a culture of pluralism.

> There are, however, certain hazards. The description of the parties may seem to presuppose some metaphysical conception of the person, for example, that the essential nature of persons is independent of and prior to their contingent attributes, including their final ends and attachments, and indeed, their character as a whole. But this is an illusion caused by not seeing the original position as a device of representation. The veil of ignorance, to mention one prominent feature of that position, has no metaphysical implications concerning the nature of the self.[9]

However, the overlapping consensus is not a mere "modus vivendi" which depends on a happy conjunction of contingencies and interests. It is based more securely on shared democratic ideals and values which form the political capital of democratic societies.[10]

The "general conception" of justice chosen unanimously under the above conditions would be the following:[11]

> All social values—liberty and opportunity, income and wealth and the bases of self-respect—are to be distributed equally unless an unequal distribution of any, or all, of these values is to everyone's advantage.

This general conception, which permits a tradeoff between liberty and income (for example), only applies in conditions of considerable scarcity. It is assumed that eventually conditions of moderate scarcity will apply in which case the special conception (below) obtains:[12]

I. Each person is to have an equal right to the most extensive total system of equal basic liberties compatible with a similar system of liberty for all.

II. Social and economic inequalities are to be arranged so that they are both:

   (a) to the greatest benefit of the least advantaged ("MAXI-MIN"), consistent with the just savings principle, and

   (b) attached to offices and positions open to all under conditions of fair equality of opportunity.

The first principle is lexically (serially) prior to the second; it is not possible for anyone to bargain rights guaranteed under (I.) for benefits that would come under (II.). This priority rule is not justified until section 82 where Rawls claims that the marginal benefit of the primary goods other than liberty is less than the marginal benefit of liberty once the basic wants have been met. Liberty is so important because it is necessary for persons to pursue their diverse ends, and it is the primary basis of self-respect. This lexical ordering has been a point of contention since it seems to at least imply a substantive conception of the good (which Rawls wants to avoid), and because conceptions of the good which some persons may hold would reverse this order.[13] Also, the principle of justice is lexically prior to the principle of efficiency (Pareto optimality), and fair opportunity (II.b) is prior to the difference principle (II.a). Justice exists by virtue of these important procedural principles of justice without direct control of individual outcomes.

Equal basic liberties, social and economic inequalities, combined with equality of opportunity (not result) and the insistence that the benefits from social cooperation serve the least advantaged, are each basic commitments of liberal democracies. Rawls's theory does offer a philosophical justification for the modern welfare state.[14] Of course, satisfying the difference principle in that context will require serious efforts at income redistribution by the state. The goal of maximizing the benefit to the least advantaged would require redistribution far beyond anything discussed in the previous chapter. It is this perspective, admittedly carried to an extreme, that characterized our participant's perspective in the 1992 presidential debate.

Evaluation

The first recognition here must be that we cannot let Rawls so easily off the hook when he claims that his theory contains no metaphysical conception of the person, but is only a device of representation for reaching an ethical consensus. It is true that Rawls has left open the task of constructing a complete anthropology, that is, Rawls allows religious and other groups, which adhere to various traditions and which have a fuller conception of the good and a substantive understanding of the human person, to affirm (or not affirm) his theory on the basis of their own convictions. Yet what remains is a skeletal philosophical anthropology. The skeletal philosophical anthropology is to an elaborated anthropology as the thin theory of the good is to a thick theory of the good. Rawls's skeletal anthropology is the decisive ethical vantage point from which to construct the fundamental principles of justice. As such, it must itself be evaluated and cannot be declared to be beyond analysis.

In a most important series of articles, Harlan Beckley[15] argues on anthropological grounds in favor of an affirmation of *A Theory of Justice* from a Christian perspective. Beckley understands (correctly) that *A Theory of Justice* deals with the formation of a moral consensus in the circumstance of modern pluralism.[16] The dilemma which Christians face in *A Theory of Justice* is, how can they really be faithful to their distinctive beliefs without forcing those who do not accept these beliefs to accept them and comply with their practical implications.[17] Beckley, relying on Gene Outka's[18] study in which agape is understood as equal regard, argues that "the distinctively Christian moral ideal of love obligates those who adhere to it to embrace the beliefs which undergird John Rawls's idea of justice as fairness. They are thereby obligated to accept something like Rawls's original position as a perspective for justifying principles of justice."[19]

Beckley points out that *A Theory of Justice* only deals with questions of distributive justice as determined in the basic structures of society. Distributive justice is not the whole of justice, and justice is certainly not the whole of morality. There is therefore room for Christian social ethics to operate in the areas of individual morality and in the matter of public goods so long as there is compliance with the basic structure. Furthermore, entering the original position will require that Christians (and others) bracket their full conception of the good only because "the restrictions of the original position seem reasonable and assist us, after reflection, in correcting or affirming the judgments we already hold."[20] Indeed, for Beckley one only accepts the restrictions of the original position because these restrictions seem acceptable *in light of* our convictions.

For Beckley, Christians can affirm *A Theory of Justice* because in the original position it "embodies a partial conception of the good which includes support for a basic structure of society that treats all persons as free, rational, and equal."[21] For Rawls, *rationality* in the original position implies that the participants do seek to maximize their expectations for primary goods, but do not know about (and consequently cannot base principles of justice on) their conception of the good. Therefore:[22]

> Basing the principles of justice on a particular conception of the good, e.g., pleasure, some notion of excellence, the Kingdom of God, would be tantamount to treating those with different conceptions as irrational.

Committed to the moral ideal of love, Christians must respect the rational moral interest of nonagapists in rules governing the basic structure of society.

There is the problem of those for whom agape requires asceticism or altruism since they may object to the concept of rationality understood as the desire for primary goods. This objection is overcome when we realize that even ascetics do not escape the need for material means to sustain life and achieve their chosen ends. Ascetics and altruists are also quite free to enforce their will over the range of goods allocated to them; asceticism and altruism are not to be equated with disinterest in how goods are distributed.[23] Furthermore, such persons remain free "to shape institutions in order to nourish the character traits they deem worthy."[24]

For Rawls, moral persons are *free* in the senses that they cannot be forced to accept principles of justice which do not serve their interests (hence the need for universal agreement in the original position) and they are free to hold or revise conceptions of the good as they see fit. It would be a violation of agape if Christians would violate the integrity and moral capacities of others by enforcing some conception of justice based on beliefs not held by others.

Finally, moral persons are *equal* as they must bargain behind a veil of ignorance in the original position. As Beckley sees it, the Rawlsian insistence on a basic equality is the strongest reason for Christians to affirm *A Theory of Justice.*[25] Agape demands equal regard; the welfare of all persons must be evaluated equally without regard to differences in social or natural contingencies (wealth, status, talent, and so forth). Those who stand within the liberal and/or Christian traditions can give some affirmation to *A Theory of Justice* on the basis of an understanding of the human person as free, equal, and rational.

L. Gregory Jones[26] responds critically to Beckley's series of articles. If we appeal to the possibility of forming an overlapping consensus where conceptions of the good are important, we are confronted with the real dilemma of contemporary society. Relying in part on the work of Alasdair MacIntyre,[27] Jones claims that an overlapping consensus will be impossible to achieve because of the moral bankruptcy of contemporary society:[28]

> The problem is that Rawls's idea of an overlapping consensus, and hence the resolution of Beckley's dilemma, is contingent on the extent to which an overlapping consensus can be shown to exist. An assessment of contemporary culture may well show that Beckley's dilemma and Rawls's overall project represent a misdiagnosis of our problem. It may be that it is not that religious beliefs and competing conceptions of the good have precluded rational agreement about the good, but rather that our institutions (and our theories which give primacy to institutions) have so corrupted our shared social practices that we no longer have the character by which we could reach some level of agreement about, as well as to embody, principles of justice.

Jones cites the Christian doctrine of sin and claims that it has robbed us of our capacity for justice. Modern institutions have corrupted our social practices and must be thoroughly critiqued so that a new vision of institutions and practices can be provided. It is through our social practices that people are formed in the virtues needed to establish and maintain just institutions, and here Christians should provide vision and example.[29]

> I believe (and Professor Beckley would, I think, agree) that the most important task for Christians committed to justice (as we must be) is to sustain the practices of justice which are in our heritage: feeding the hungry, clothing the naked, serving the widow, ensuring that people of all nations have access to essential "primary goods," and the like. Such activity is central to Christian life, and we ought to participate in those practices which will enable the virtue of justice to flourish.

Jones has argued that Christians ethics has its own distinct content and vision, and fidelity to these does not point to participation in the original position.

To conclude, for Beckley Christians can affirm *A Theory of Justice* based on the Christian concept of agape. On the basis of agape and in a pluralistic context, we expect Christians to treat all persons as free, rational, and equal. This clearly contributes to, but does not summarize, a proper Christian anthropology. We could, for example, easily cite many instances in which these very liberal conceptions have informed and influenced Catholic Social Thought. The contribution made by the American Jesuit John Courtney Murray in the area of religious liberty is an instance of a distinctively American commitment to freedom of conscience and thought which has entered into the Catholic understanding of the human person. The document of the Second Vatican Council, *Dignitatis Humanae,* was of course quite revolutionary. Furthermore, women have made, and we hope will continue to make, important gains under the banner of "equality" within Catholic institutions and practices. Beckley is, in my view, quite correct about the positive correlation between Rawlsian anthropology and the proper Christian understanding of the human person. Furthermore, included in Beckley's view is the expectation that people do have fuller visions of the human person and that these supplement the Rawlsian understanding.[30] These fuller visions are preserved in and through those groups which mediated between the individual and the larger society; the churches most especially contribute here. Of course, if in practice these groups do not preserve the fuller vision because they have given up the task or have themselves been eroded in their public significance, then our understanding of the human person is impoverished, and with this our ethical constructs are crippled.

The limited anthropology of "free, rational, and equal" has also been an albatross. Jones and other virtue theorists point out that in fact this limited anthropology is not being supplemented with a fuller vision of human character, virtue, and personhood, but has tragically come to occupy all or most of what we understand to characterize the human person. We may summarize Jones for our purposes by saying that the Rawlsian anthropology omits or slights features of human personhood and existence which include human sociality, spiritual aspirations, finitude, and sin. What follows are deleterious consequences for human existence which Christians seek to remedy through "feeding the hungry, clothing the naked, serving the widow, ensuring that people of all nations have access to essential 'primary goods,' " and other acts which seek a more just order.

Finally, precisely because *A Theory of Justice* deals with questions of distributive justice as determined in the basic structures of society, we must also recognize the possibility of statism and the devastating consequences for human agency which would concern all of our theological ethicists. By statism we mean a situation in which excessive authority and responsibility are vested in the state; this possibility haunts the theory as the central authority is charged with accomplishing the second principle of justice which regulates the (strongly egalitarian) distribution of primary goods. Ronald Nash[31] in particular criticizes Rawls for the extent to which the state will have to be involved in economic life in order to satisfy the principles of justice.

Michael Walzer

Walzer's work *Spheres of Justice*[32] is a response to the monumental work *A Theory of Justice*. Walzer also builds a theory of justice based on the anthropological pillars of liberty and equality; but to this he adds a much stronger emphasis on human sociality. For Walzer, humans are social by nature; the choice to enter into relations with others is not a decision made by an already fully formed, self-sufficient, autonomous individual.

The abstractness of Rawls detaches us from many of the contingencies of life upon which moral decisions are in fact made. Walzer on the other hand seems more true to the complexity involved in the distribution of different goods. To Walzer's mind, philosophers must learn to resist the temptations to search for some short list of basic goods (as does Rawls with his definition of "primary goods") and then to offer a single distributive criterion for distribution ("maximin").

The theory of goods lays the groundwork for the entire theory of justice. Goods are items that are socially valued (not just idiosyncratically valued); they participate in the identity formation of individuals; goods considered primary will certainly tend to vary across cultures; goods are distributed according to their social meaning; different social meanings necessitate different and autonomous spheres of distribution. Injustice (also called tyranny) happens when one good (capital, office, land, etc.) becomes monopolized, and the monopolists then invade and dominate other distributive spheres. For example, control of capital must not translate into dominance in the political sphere. Political influence must not be distributed according to the mode of an alien sphere. This is to distribute political influence against its (social) meaning. Walzer describes how this comes about:[33]

> Physical strength, familial reputation, religious or political office, landed wealth, capital, technical knowledge: each of these, in different historical periods, has been dominant; and each of them has been monopolized by some group of men and women. And then all good things come to those who have the one best thing. Possess that one, and the others come in train. Or, to change the metaphor, a dominant good is converted into another good, into many others, in accordance with what often appears to be a natural process but is in fact magical, a kind of social alchemy.

Therefore, unlike Rawls, Walzer has a two-fold attack against monopoly. Not only must we work to bring about more equality (Rawls), but we must also combat the dominance of any one good or set of goods.

Justice is plural since different goods must be distributed for different reasons. Each good has its own proper distributive sphere in this sense. A single rule or set of rules cannot cover all goods. Of special concern to us is his discussion of "commodities." Ordinary commodities may indeed be distributed according to market criteria. Market criteria cannot however infringe on "needed goods" which are in the domain of rights. These are distributed in an egalitarian way. There are other exchanges which are not done solely or at all according to market criteria; they include the buying and selling of: people (slavery), political power, criminal justice, freedoms of speech, religion, etc., marriage rights, military service requirements, divine grace, etc. Walzer relies on economist Arthur Okun for his articulation of "blocked exchanges."[34]

Walzer then, by defining various spheres of distribution, has left us with some version of a market which operates largely according to utilitarian considerations. He would however more to break up market monopolies and most importantly to restrict the dominance of the market mentality in our society. His many suggestions for society in general are summed up as follows:[35]

> The appropriate arrangements in our own society are those, I think, of a decentralized democratic socialism; a strong welfare state run, in part at least, by local and amateur officials; a constrained market; an open and demystified civil service; independent public schools; the sharing of hard work and free time; the protection of religious and familial life; a system of public honoring and dishonoring free from all considerations of rank or class; workers' control of companies and factories; a politics of parties, movements, meetings, and public debate.

Evaluation

Like Rawls, Walzer develops a theory of justice based on the freedom and equality of individuals in society. Very positively, Walzer reminds us more clearly about the communitarian strands within the liberal tradition. Furthermore, Walzer does justice to pluralism across different goods and across different cultures in a way that Rawls does not. His work accords with the way people do and must make decisions in the context of their community in which people share *membership*. There are however important questions.

A theory of goods lays the groundwork for the entire theory of justice. This raises two problems. Such a theory is inherently and radically relativist since the social valuation of goods is assumed to vary across cultures, and no criteria are offered which might make it possible to criticize any particular social valuation of a good.[36] Second, but related to the first objection, goods (material and nonmaterial) and not the human person are the foundation for how institutions and practices are guided.

Walzer has no grounds on which to criticize the social valuation of any particular good. There is no basis on which to say that some uses of our scarce resources serve the human person better than others. Christian ethics cannot simply accept the existing valuation of various goods and concern itself only with what seem to be the attendant principles of distribution. Our actual valuations of various goods will evidence the reality of original sin. Christian ethics has always contained value systems in which certain goods might legitimately be encouraged, such as housing, food, health care, rigorous education, while some might be pursued more conservatively. Arguable examples of these are luxury goods, nuclear weapons, and goods that involve pollution.

We move now from consideration of distribution-related questions within *Spheres of Justice* to consideration of production-related questions. Walzer severely downplays individual ownership rights in those goods which have been produced by one's own labor. For many goods, especially those which fall into the category of need, distribution is to occur according to the social valuation of that good relatively independently of the production process. This raises the question of the legitimate extent of ownership rights. Furthermore, if we have an understanding of human motivation which appreciates the need for incentives in the process of production, we see that there is also an efficiency issue at stake here. The exigencies of production are important reasons for the dominance of the market.

Walzer relies on Okun for that part of his analysis which concerns the market, but it seems that Okun's most basic purpose in writing has been short changed.[37] Certainly the thrust of Okun's work is that the designation of rights and the distribution according to nonmarket criteria entails inefficiency (loss in total output). The method of distribution will affect production, so we have a tradeoff situation. Yet

Walzer never considers the issue of efficiency adequately in his discussion of justice.

There is no explicit consideration of the problem of efficiency anywhere in the work. To be fair, I do believe that there is an implied appreciation for the problem in the overall project of boundary maintenance between the various spheres which coincide with appropriate criteria for just distribution. This project protects both pluralism and some concept of a *limited* state. Unfortunately, state takeover of distributive justice only where the goods may be considered necessities implies to me at least an unacceptable expansion of the powers of the state. Health care, housing, food, and clothing must surely be considered among human basic needs which Walzer would not leave within the domain of the market for the purposes of distribution. Consider now that consumer spending[38] in 1994 for health care was $834 billion (18 percent of all personal consumption expenditures), total housing $1,235 billion (26 percent), food $716 billion (15 percent), clothing, excluding jewelry, $274 billion (5.8 percent). These sum to 64.8 percent of *all* personal consumption expenditures. Because we are speaking about a potentially large portion of the GNP, Walzer would have to explain much more theoretically and empirically before one could be confident that his solution is not a statist one.

Following Okun, I would say that it is a matter of efficiency to give the producer of a product some claim over what (s)he has invested labor in, and not to distribute solely according to norms internal to the good itself. Following Locke, I would say that it is a matter of justice to give the producer of a product some claim over what (s)he has invested labor in. And again, although Walzer does work on a basic understanding of humans as free and equal, his theory quickly removes the person from the center of justice and places the social meaning of material goods there in place. Finally, we can only ponder with fear and trepidation the attendant theory and size of the state which follows from Walzer's theory of justice and the enforcement of the proper rules of distribution in the various spheres.

Robert Nozick

Nozick's work *Anarchy, State, and Utopia*[39] is a libertarian response to the monumental work *A Theory of Justice*. Nozick is primarily concerned with questions about justice and the state. For Nozick, the moral status of the state and of social arrangements in general depends on compliance with the individual right against noninterference. Liberty and equality are also anthropological pillars for this theory. However, while Rawls stressed equality, Nozick consistently stresses liberty.

In his examination of questions about the legitimacy of the state, Nozick relies heavily on the state of nature theory of John Locke. In part one of the book, Nozick argues that it is possible to justify the existence of a minimal state. In part two he argues that it is not possible to justify more than the minimal state. Finally, in part three he argues that these conclusions are not unhappy ones. Central to the theory is the idea that individuals have an absolute right to nonaggression by others. Nonaggression against other persons is the necessary moral side constraint on all action. The fact that persons shape life individually to find meaning is the special trait that demands treatment according to the moral side constraint.

The state of nature theory is advantageous in settling questions about the legitimacy of the state. It is advantageous because we can examine whether the existence of a state would be superior to a situation of anarchy and whether the establishment of a state would involve morally impermissible steps. Second, the state of nature theory allows us to understand the political realm in terms of the nonpolitical. It has an expository function. (See table 3.1.)

The situation of individuals in Locke's state of nature gives persons "freedom to order their actions and dispose of their possessions and persons as they think fit, within the bounds of the law of nature", but this situation is subject to many serious inconveniences. In a situation of anarchy, it will be difficult to see to the enforcement on one's rights. Groups of individuals will tend to form mutual protection agencies where all will answer the call of any member for defense or for the enforcement of his rights. For practical reasons, one agency will emerge as dominant within a geographic area through an invisible-hand process which violates nobody's rights. This dominant protective agency is like a state, but it is not a state. While the dominant protective agency now has a practical monopoly on force, membership is not universal. So, it may be called an ultraminimal state.

After the system of many private protective agencies has given way

Table 3.1   The Development of the Minimal State

Authorities	Monopoly on Force	Universal Membership
Private Protective Associations	NO	NO
Ultraminimal State	YES	NO
Minimal State (Night Watchmen State)	YES	YES

to the ultraminimal state by an invisible-hand process, Nozick claims that the emergence of the minimal state will happen by moral necessity. The minimal state will provide benefits of protection even to those who cannot afford to pay. The problem now is to show that the necessary redistribution to accomplish this is legitimate.

The dominant protective agency may punish unreliable punishers (other agencies) as authorized by its members to do so.[40] Because of the risk of violating rights that some activities entail, there can be cause for prohibiting these activities. According to the principle of compensation, persons disadvantaged by having their liberty reduced because of the risk involved in activities to which they have a right must be compensated. The dominant protective agency will prohibit defective agencies from punishing its members although members of defective agencies have a right to see to punishment of guilty offenders. Therefore members of unreliable agencies must be compensated. This compensation takes the form of protective services against its own clients to those disadvantaged by the prohibition. Now we have a minimal state, and this ends Nozick's argument in part one.

In part two Nozick argues that it is not possible to justify more than the minimal state which would involve redistribution of personal holdings. In chapter 7 of part two he discusses his theory of "just holdings" (instead of the loaded term "distributive justice"):

1. A person who acquires a holding in accordance with the principle of justice in acquisition is entitled to that holding.
2. A person who acquires a holding in accordance with the principle of justice in transfer, from someone else entitled to the holding, is entitled to the holding.

3. No one is entitled to a holding except by (repeated) applications of 1 and 2.

Just acquisition comes about when labor is mixed with an object subject to the proviso that there be "enough and as good left in common for others."[41] The market does not generally violate this proviso in the sense of worsening another's situation by depriving him/her of something he/she otherwise would possess. Justice in transfer requires mutual agreement by two parties in a market transaction. However, the above principles are subject to the principle of rectification which would require a rearrangement of holdings in the light of past injustices. Nozick mentions the need for such a principle but unfortunately does not pursue it. This theory of holdings (also called "the entitlement theory") rejects a redistribution to bring about a pattern of holdings (such as one of equality) more to the liking of the state. Nozick's approach is historical, and not end state. The distribution of holdings is a result of past activity and is not reformed in the end to suit some policymakers' preferences. End-state patterns fail to understand that goods do not exist as manna from heaven. Goods come into the world with a claim resulting from the very process of the production of those goods.

This approach would rule out those of John Rawls and Michael Walzer. Rawls distributes goods according to his formula of serving the least advantaged, while Walzer distributes goods according to the internal dynamics of a specific good, neglecting historical entitlements. Though Nozick does not specifically mention Walzer here, his comments are directed against his school of thought:

> ... why must the internal goal of the activity take precedence over, for example, the person's particular purpose in performing the activity? ... Why must his [a doctor's] activities be allocated via the internal goal of medical care? It seems clear that he needn't do that; just because he has this skill, why should he bear the costs of the desired allocation, why is he less entitled to pursue his own goals within the special circumstances of practicing medicine, than everyone else?

Indeed, any attempt to maintain some (ahistorical) pattern of holdings necessarily violates liberty. To demonstrate this Nozick offers a highly entertaining and compelling example (Nozick, pp.160–64) worth summarizing here. Suppose that you are the happy policymaker whose nonentitlement conception for a distribution of holdings is finally realized, call it D1. Suppose even that the existing distribution is your favorite one. Now suppose that Wilt Chamberlain, a large gate attraction, signs a contract for a large sum of money with the local team. Ticket prices go up slightly to pay for his salary as fans happily pay to see him play basketball. Chamberlain now has a much larger income and bank account than anyone else. Is the new distribution, D2, unjust? And if so, why? There is no doubt that those resources voluntarily transferred to Chamberlain were under the legitimate control of the people who did so since holdings under D1 (your favorite distribution) were thought to be legitimate. Clearly, no end-state principle can be continuously realized without continuous redistribution by the state or by a law forbidding capitalist acts between consenting adults. The more-than-minimal state must violate liberty.

Part three contains a discussion of the idea of utopia. Nozick offers no substantive definition of what a utopia might look like. He does offer a "framework for utopia" though. Communities are established which people may freely join. Some central authority, equivalent to the minimal state, is necessary to regulate the relations between communities, but the internal affairs are regulated internally and vary among communities. The framework works something like a marketplace of communities where people vote with their feet. Through an evolutionary process, the less desirable communities are filtered out and only the best emerge. The best emerge not according to any plan or design, but through this process of filtering out as members leave and some models eventually fail. If there is anything as a single best utopia, it will emerge. More likely, though, different communities will suit different persons. The utopia problem does not have a unique solution.

Evaluation

Like Rawls in his theory of justice, Nozick seeks to do justice to the reality of our separate existences. For Rawls, this rules out utilitarianism. For Nozick, this rules out any collective action that is not explicitly based on an established agreement on the part of those affected. Personal liberty (understood in an individualistic way) is the supreme value which may not be violated. We must all act according to this "moral side constraint" in our dealings with others. The fact that persons shape life individually to find meaning is the special trait which demands behavior according to the moral side constraint.

Nozick's discussion of the "experience machine" contains an illuminating discussion about the execution of a life plan by a rational being with the capacity to shape her or his life in order to strive for a meaningful life. Nozick asks us to imagine an "experience machine" that would give you any experience you desired:

> Superduper neuropsychologists could stimulate your brain so that you would think and feel you were writing a great novel, or making a friend, or reading an interesting book. All the time you would be floating in a tank, with electrodes attached to your brain. Should you plug into this machine for life, preprogramming your life's experiences? . . . *What else can matter to us, other than how our lives feel from the inside?* [Italics in original]
>
> We learn that something matters to us in addition to experience by imagining an experience machine and then realizing that we would not use it.[42]

Nozick concludes his thought experiment by suggesting that what we really desire "is to live (an active verb) ourselves, in contact with reality."[43] A person does not want to be an "indeterminate blob." There is clearly a human good beyond the experience of pleasure.

For John Finnis,[44] Nozick's experiment demonstrates important though indirect connections with the Thomistic Aristotelian Tradition in which persons achieve their perfection through action. The development and maintenance of one's identity is an important human good, and it is formed through free choices. "One's free choices go to constitute oneself, so that one's own character or identity is the most fundamental of one's 'accomplishments.' "[45] Furthermore, Nozick's great contribution in the present context is that it brings us to consideration of the concept of subsidiarity. As Finnis states, "the twentieth century German Jesuits who formulated the principle of subsidiarity—that principle of justice which insists that people should not be absorbed into giant enterprises in which they are mere cogs without opportunity to act on their own initiative—found their inspiration in the neo-Aristotelian tag, *omne ens perficitur in actu:* flourishing is to be found in action.[46] Of course, from our perspective greater insight into the social nature of the human person would be necessary before Nozick could embrace this concept which presupposes an agent who acts in community with others.

There are many arrangements in life that may appropriately be viewed as simple matters of agreement between free individuals. Even Walzer admits this much. Behavior in the marketplace is governed this way. But if there is to be true human fulfillment, the market must know some bounds just as liberty must know some bounds. If Nozick really takes seriously his brief discussion about persons shaping life to find meaning, then I think that he would be forced to admit a host of other person-centered concerns which enter into the pursuit of meaning:[47]

> Why not interfere with someone else's shaping of his own life? . . . I conjecture that the answer is connected with that elusive and difficult notion: the meaning of life. A person's shaping his life in accordance with some overall plan is his way of giving meaning to his life; only a being with the capacity to so shape his life can have or strive for meaningful life.

The finding of personal meaning and fulfillment would surely include greater recognition of the social nature of the human person and the role played by all of us in meeting the bodily and spiritual needs of one another. Furthermore, the reality of original sin indicates that there should be some social and institutional assistance offered in helping a person shape his/her life in accordance with authentic goals.

Conclusion

The worthy pillars of a liberal anthropology are liberty, equality, and rationality. However, the noted deficiencies in the philosophical anthropologies cause the theories of justice to vacillate between statism (Rawls and Walzer) and libertarianism (Nozick). Any Christian Personalist theory in dialogue with contemporary liberalism must show appreciation for these insights as well as attempt to correct weaknesses. That will be the agenda of chapter 4.

As noted earlier, Rawls and Nozick in particular have produced leading works in analytical moral philosophy which mirror at a scholarly level the dominant political perspectives in American policy formation today.[48] The inability of market forces left alone to meet at least the basic needs of all according to our equal human dignity has been the rationale for the state to intervene. This intervention in turn generates disturbances in personal rights, initiative, and creativity. So the entire debate at the levels of philosophy and policy seems hopelessly ensnared in the rhetoric of libertarian freedom (a more Republican Party emphasis) vs. state intervention in pursuit of a basic equality (a more Democratic Party emphasis).

The data of chapter 2 and chapter 3 are mutually illuminating. Chapter 2 is the experiential evidence of the issues, explored more theoretically in chapter 3. Precisely because the maintenance of full human agency became a problem under statist solutions to social problems in which "distributive justice" was the primary battle cry, recent reforms in the welfare state have come to stress decentralization and decategorization which yield a greater sphere of action and responsibility to more local levels.

In recent times, liberalism has produced a variety of answers to the question about the proper role for the state. We have seen that the economic liberalism of the nineteenth century, fascism in Italy and Germany, and even communism may be considered a product of (or reaction to) this liberal dilemma. The United States is now wrestling with precisely this dilemma in its own way and context. There is cause for hope, given the growing appreciation described in chapter 2, that exists both in Washington and in the country at large, concerning the importance of local initiative by community-based organizations in the formation of social policy. In any case, the proper balance or antidote to this statism is not further emphasis on the isolated individual, but an expanded understanding of the human person which accounts for human agency in the context of our varied social communities. We must add to, transform, and build upon the three great pillars of a liberal anthropology. The maintenance of social equity, initiative, and creativity are attainable only in this way.

In the coming chapters we shall see how the interpretation of

Catholic Social Thought to be developed here offers an expanded anthropological perspective as the measure by which to assess the merits of social arrangements and to set a social moral agenda. Furthermore, it is with the principle of subsidiarity and through participation in culture that persons must find the all important fuller vision of the good spoken about by Rawls.

Notes

1. Michael Novak, *Free Persons and the Common Good* (New York: Madison Books, 1989), p.172.
2. Alasdair MacIntyre, *After Virtue* (Notre Dame, Indiana: University of Notre Dame Press, 1981), ch.17.
3. Robert Nozick, *Anarchy, State, and Utopia* (New York: Basic Books, 1974), p.183.
4. John Rawls, *A Theory of Justice* (Cambridge, Massachusetts: Belknap Press of Harvard University Press, 1971), p.7.
5. These things are later called the "thin theory of the good" (Rawls, *A Theory of Justice*, p.396) since they are essential to fulfill a rational life plan. The full theory of the good requires the use of the principles of justice (p.433). Rawls notes that in his contract theory, in contrast to utilitarianism, the good is defined subsequent to the right.
6. From the first appearance of *A Theory of Justice*, the basis for the list has been in question. It seems to represent a very culturally bound and Western understanding of a good life and not to be a thin theory about the good at all. See: Robert Wolff, *Understanding Rawls* (Princeton, New Jersey: Princeton University Press, 1977).
7. Rawls, *A Theory of Justice*, p.131.
8. Michael Sandel, *Liberalism and the Limits of Justice* (Cambridge, England: Cambridge University Press, 1982).
9. John Rawls, "Justice as Fairness: Political Not Metaphysical," *Philosophy and Public Affairs*, summer 1985, p.238.
10. John Rawls, "The Idea of an Overlapping Consensus," *Oxford Journal of Legal Studies*, vol. 7, 1987, pp.1–25.
11. Rawls, *A Theory of Justice*, p.62.
12. Rawls, *A Theory of Justice*, p.302.
13. Rex Martin correctly points out that the backdrop of Rawls's contract theory is the inability of utilitarianism to generate an adequate account of basic moral and constitutional rights. For Martin, Rawls has made his case that rights (as a group) would be preferred over other aggrega-

tive concerns. However, the added argument for the priority of liberty is weak and perhaps factually wrong. See: Rex Martin, *Rawls and Rights* (Lawrence, Kansas: University of Kansas Press, 1985). I believe that the difficulties Rawls has in giving a satisfactory justification for the primary goods and for the lexical ordering of the principles of justice seem to indicate the need for a more substantive theory of the good.

14. Indeed, Rawls develops his theory in the second section of *A Theory of Justice* using the backdrop of a constitutional democracy much resembling Western democracies.

15. Harlan R. Beckley, "A Christian Affirmation of Rawls's Idea of Justice as Fairness—Part 1," *Journal of Religious Ethics,* vol. 13, fall 1985, pp.210–42.

    Harlan R. Beckley, "A Christian Affirmation of Rawls's Idea of Justice as Fairness—Part 2," *Journal of Religious Ethics,* vol. 14, fall 1986, pp.229–46.

16. For Rawls:

    > Liberalism as a political doctrine supposes that there are many conflicting and incommensurable conceptions of the good, each compatible with the full rationality of human persons. The historical origin of this liberal supposition is the Reformation and its consequences. One task of liberalism as a political doctrine is to answer the question: how is social unity to be understood, given that there can be no public agreement on the one rational good, and a plurality of opposing and incommensurable conceptions must be taken as given?

    Rawls, "Justice as Fairness: Political Not Metaphysical," pp.248–9.

17. Beckley rejects views of Christian ethics in which this question would not even arise. He rejects the view that there are no distinctive Christian principles or obligations which can be associated with Christian beliefs (as represented in the work of Arthur J. Dyck). In a similar way, he does not accept the opposite extreme view that there are no points of contact between Christian ethics and non-Christian ethics (as represented by John H. Yoder). If one is committed to either view, it is clear that the issue of an affirmation of a philosophical treatise on justice by persons with a distinctive Christian ethic will never arise. Following James Gustafson, Beckley does accept the view that there are distinctive (though not unique) Christian principles which arise on the basis of experience in a Christian community, yet there is continuity with ethics done from other perspectives.

18. Gene Outka, *Agape: An Ethical Analysis* (New Haven: Yale University Press, 1972).

19. Beckley, "A Christian Affirmation of Rawls's Idea of Justice as Fairness—Part 1," p.212.
20. Beckley, "A Christian Affirmation of Rawls's Idea of Justice as Fairness—Part 1," p.232.
21. Beckley, "A Christian Affirmation of Rawls's Idea of Justice as Fairness—Part 1," p.231.
22. Beckley, "A Christian Affirmation of Rawls's Idea of Justice as Fairness—Part 1," p.234.
23. Such criticism has been made in a very helpful way by Richard Fern, "Religious Belief in a Rawlsian Society," *Journal of Religious Ethics* 15, spring 1987, pp.33–58. Fern distinguishes two categories of religious persons who are potentially disadvantaged by institutions formed according to Rawlsian justice. First, there are those who follow an altruistic interpretation of the Gospel in which persons must be radically nonassertive concerning their own needs. To this objection Beckley has responded directly and well as I describe above. Second, there are those for whom absolute commitment disallows any morality outside of their distinctive ethic, as exemplified in the teaching that "no one who puts his hand to the plough and then looks back, is fitted for the Kingdom of God." Certainly few Christians would interpret fidelity to their beliefs as a necessary rejection of all values not explicitly theologically derived. Rather, what seems to be required is that Christians show fidelity to their ultimate commitments and that other systems of ethics be understood as serving only a subordinate function. Of course, Beckley's answer here is delivered in the context of his overall position. Beckley makes his case using a particular interpretation of agape which permits participation in the original position for a people whose situation is characterized by legitimate pluralism. Not all interpretations of Christian ethics are covered. Beckley readily recognizes this limitation (Beckley, 1986, p.241).
24. Beckley, "A Christian Affirmation of Rawls's Idea of Justice as Fairness—Part 2," p.243.
25. Beckley, "A Christian Affirmation of Rawls's Idea of Justice as Fairness—Part 2," p.237.
26. L. Gregory Jones, "Should Christians Affirm Rawls's Justice as Fairness? A Response to Professor Beckley," *Journal of Religious Ethics,* fall 1988, vol. 16, pp.251–71.
27. Jones makes use of the critiques of liberal society to be found in Alasdair MacIntyre, *After Virtue* (Notre Dame, Indiana: University of Notre Dame Press, 1981); MacIntyre, *Whose Justice? Which Rationality?* (Notre Dame, Indiana: University of Notre Dame Press, 1988).

28. Jones, "Should Christians Affirm Rawls's Justice as Fairness? A Response to Professor Beckley," p.260.
29. Jones, "Should Christians Affirm Rawls's Justice as Fairness? A Response to Professor Beckley," p.268.
30. This caveat is of vital significance. In later chapters we shall see how essential the principle of subsidiarity is in this regard.
31. Ronald Nash, *Social Justice and the Christian Church* (Milford, Michigan: Mott Media, 1983).
32. Michael Walzer, *Spheres of Justice* (New York: Basic Books, 1983).
33. Walzer, *Spheres of Justice*, p.11.
34. Walzer, *Spheres of Justice*, p.100.
35. Walzer, *Spheres of Justice*, p.318.
36. Individuals in the "original position" were assumed to be free, equal, and also rational. It is this emphasis on rationality, which is not found in Walzer, that allows Rawls to escape relativism.
37. A.M. Okun, *Equality and Efficiency—the Big Tradeoff* (Washington, D.C.: Brookings Institution, 1975).
    Okun, "Further Thoughts on Equality and Efficiency," in J. Pechman (ed.), *Economics for Policymaking* (Cambridge, Massachusetts: MIT Press, 1983).
38. U.S. Bureau of the Census, *Statistical Abstract of the United States: 1997*, Washington, D.C. Table no. 702.
39. Nozick, 1974.
40. No agency can aggregate any rights to itself not explicitly given to it by its members.
41. Nozick, *Anarchy, State, and Utopia*, p.175.
42. Nozick, *Anarchy, State, and Utopia*, pp.42–4.
43. Nozick, *Anarchy, State, and Utopia*, p.45.
44. John Finnis, *Fundamentals of Ethics* (Washington, D.C.: Georgetown University Press, 1983).
45. Finnis, *Fundamentals of Ethics*, p.40.
46. Finnis, *Fundamentals of Ethics*, p.39.
47. Nozick, *Anarchy, State, and Utopia*, p.50.
48. I would suggest that the philosophical underpinnings of the Democratic Party platform resonate well with the Rawlsian perspective. I would make the same comment about the Republican Party and Nozick.

4

Toward a New Synthesis: Christian Personalism and Democratic Capitalism

> In the developed countries there is a poverty of intimacy, a poverty of spirit, of loneliness, of lack of love. There is no greater sickness in the world today than that one. — Mother Theresa

The central task of an economic system is to meet human needs and simultaneously to provide for the development of human beings. A major reality and certainly the dominant problem from the moral perspective of the American system is the persistence of terrible need in a "prosperous" land, and the lack of full personal development. In previous chapters we have credited democratic capitalism with extraordinary productivity, and we have noted its distributional inequities. The shortcomings of the applied ethical theory and technical efforts to reduce these inequities have challenged us to come to a better understanding of the human person and human agency and constructively to expand (not replace) the social anthropology of contemporary liberal thought and practice which focus on freedom, equality, and rationality.

Christian Personalist theories applied to issues and problems relating to personal, medical, and sexual ethics have been developed extensively since the Second Vatican Council. However, recently the Christian Personalism of the council is emerging again as a powerful *social* ethical framework. It is rising to a prominence in social ethics that it has not seen since the days of the earlier Christian Personalists, including Em-

101

manuel Mounier, Gabriel Marcel, Max Scheler, and others. Michael Novak has made invaluable contributions in this endeavor.

My vision here coheres in basic perspective with what I understand to be that of contemporary Catholic Social Thought, and especially that of John Paul II. I am pursing here a critical affirmation of market institutions and practices from a Christian Personalist perspective. This critical affirmation accepts market institutions as the *basis* on which to build a more just society. I use here the term "democratic capitalism" from Michael Novak because the words immediately imply the necessity of democratic political institutions and cultural framework in guiding and at times constraining market forces.[1]

I do not claim that Personalist theory within Catholic Social Thought offers us a definitive social anthropology. By its "central affirmation of the existence of free and creative persons, Personalism always introduces into the heart of its constructions a principle of unpredictability which excludes any desire for a definitive system."[2] True to its phenomenological method, a Personalist theory worthy of the name remains open to and influenced by new events and ideas.

I follow Emmanuel Mounier in understanding Personalism not as a system, but as a perspective, method, and exigency.[3] As a perspective it places *anthropology* at its center. It sees a proper understanding of the human person as the key to progress in the struggle for social justice. Most important (for Mounier and also for Catholic Social Thought), is the fundamental nature of persons which is to aspire not to separation, but to communication with other persons.[4] As a method, Personalism is *incarnational* as it rejects methods that are purely deductive or crudely empirical. Human history must move forward to a Personalist future, but that future is not known deductively through an idea nor is it evident solely through examination of the situation. It is known and advanced through "engagement" in a situation. As exigency, Personalism demands *social action* which is prophetic, effective, leads to personal development, and promotes the common good.

Toward a Personalist Social Anthropology

For sacred scripture teaches that man was created "to the image of God," is capable of knowing and loving his Creator, and was appointed by him as master of all earthly creatures that he might subdue them and use them to God's glory. . . . God did not create man as a solitary. For from the beginning "male and female he created them" (Gen. 1:27). Their companionship produces the primary form of interpersonal communion. For by his innermost nature man is a social being, and unless he relates himself to others he can neither live nor develop his potential.[5]

Catholic Social Thought, especially since the Second Vatican Council, has in fact adopted the anthropological perspective as the defining ethical perspective. All things on earth are understood as being ordered to human beings as their center and summit.[6] Indeed, human persons are created in the very "image and likeness of God," distinguished as they are from other creatures by their capacity to know and to love. These human capacities to know and to love find their perfection in a wisdom which is oriented toward what is genuinely true and what is genuinely good. Therefore it is God alone who can offer the final fulfillment for human beings. In other words, God gives persons their true *being,* not simply in the sense of existence in time and space, but in the sense of life purpose, meaning, and ethical structure.

This God in whom persons find their fulfillment is a Trinitarian God. The Christian teaching of the Trinitarian nature of God invites us to considerations of God's unity in difference and to the process of giving and receiving love. Christians believe that God's being is not solitary, but communal. We speak of a community of persons, Father, Son, and Spirit, who give and receive the gift of love. Human persons, created in the image and likeness of God, also find their true *being* in the process of giving and receiving love and in the experience of unity amidst difference. Christian Personalism engages in a rich exploration to determine the implications of these doctrines for social ethics.

God has created persons as body and spirit, and we are oriented toward God also in our bodily composition. Personalism has an "integral anthropology." Those processes which involve us in the very material aspects of our existence should serve to reveal the hidden presence of God. Although, realistically speaking, the activities of caring for the body, providing for the needs of family and self, and participating in economic life do involve some repetition and at times toil, the more salient truth is that in the process of these activities, we can discover and recognize the activity and presence of the God who gives and receives love.

It is only in the exercise of our freedom that we can turn ourselves toward what is truly good.[7] In our freedom and creativity, we may participate in and contribute to that process of giving and receiving love that involves God and other persons. The process will naturally flourish with the multiplication of relationships that are consequent to daily living. Of course, a realistic understanding of the human person must recognize the significance of human finitude and the significance and tenacity of sin. In our finitude, we realize that we can never achieve the good that we often desire. We must learn patience, fortitude, and humility in the face of reality in setting objectives. Refusal to do this is a rejection of our bodily nature. Furthermore, in our freedom we have all refused to participate as we should in the process of giving and receiving love; the image of God in us all is thereby lessened and distorted.

Especially through cross-fertilization with liberal theory and practice, Catholic Social Thought has shown a new emphasis on human equality. Despite differences in sex, race, color, birth, and intelligence, the documents have come to stress basic human equality. We may speak of a human equality in the sense that all persons are called to know and to love God, and all have certain rights and duties with respect to other persons. The basic equality among persons has been the basis for the call to provide all persons, and especially the least advantaged, with the necessary material and nonmaterial support to achieve the ends of human life.

I want to review each of these items in order to expand our social anthropology and to draw out the implications for social ethics. We begin first with the conviction about the social nature of the human person.

The Social Nature of the Human Person

Catholic Social Thought has always rejected the individualism which characterizes the work of both Rawls and Nozick. Of course, Rawls and Nozick both agree that rationally self-interested individuals do cooperate and that they do enter into various relations with one another including families, churches, civic associations, and so forth. However, neither author understands our sociality as truly essential to a discussion of the human person. In the cases of both theories, we may speak of individual persons apart from and before they voluntarily join with others (if they do decide to join with others). This is only a superficial and sentimental understanding of our social nature. Fortunately, the work of Walzer testifies at least to the survival within liberalism of a more profound sense of our nature as social beings. Therefore, in its emphasis on communitarianism, Catholic Social Thought does not introduce something "alien" but recovers and deepens insights in human nature which are slighted today in theory and practice.

For one interpreter of Catholic Social Thought, communitarianism appears as *the* guiding source of ethical insight. Michael J. Schuck proposes his own theory in this way:

> This theory holds that papal teaching coheres around a theologically inspired communitarian social ethic which has yielded a cluster of shared, double-pulsed insights concerning religious, political, familial, economic, and cultural relations in society.[8]

The fruitful tensions (or double-pulsed insights) common to Catholic Social Thought are in essence inspired by communitarianism. For Schuck, the pastoral approach of the pre-Leonine period (1740–1877) has an image of God as Christ the Good Shepherd; the natural law approach of the Leonine period (1878–1958) has an image of God as Father-Creator; and the post-Leonine period (1959-present) has an image of God as dialogical-Spirit.[9] These perspectives are linked in a communitarian understanding of the will of God for humankind:

> The Shepherd's ingathering, the unity of creation, the Spirit's dialogic invitation—all communicate the 'gravitational' draw of God's will for community.[10]

I believe that Schuck has taken what is perhaps the single most salient feature of Catholic Social Thought, particularly when viewed in the light of contemporary liberalism, and used it to represent an entire

Personalist theory. Nevertheless, Schuck does correctly point out the communitarian aspects within Catholic Social Thought.

The full realization of the human person is most closely connected with a social nature. Sin is understood primarily as whatever brings the person out of harmony with God, himself/herself and others.[11] When the person seeks happiness and fulfillment apart from God and apart from others, the person lives "in darkness." Therefore, it is an end in itself requiring no further justification for us to belong to our families, neighborhoods, churches, professional associations, town communities, civic organizations, and other associations which help fulfill our social nature.

Of course, the modern world no longer offers us the sense of nearness and closeness offered by the premodern village. Fortunately, Catholic Social Thought does not require that we lament the loss of these little lost communities. Since Leo XIII, Catholic Social Thought has strongly supported many of the emerging new forms of associations, the modern labor union being an important example. In this spirit contemporary interpreters of Catholic Social Thought and modern life ask us to consider positively the new but as yet unappreciated new forms of community:

> I do not think that *anyone* has grasped clearly enough the spiritual ideal behind the new forms of voluntary association—the new communitarian ideal—involved in liberal societies.
>
> The most distinctive invention of the spirit of capitalism is not the individual as much as it is many individuals joining together in creative enterprise. It is, for example, the joint stock company, the corporation; or again, the credit union, as well as insurance funds and pension funds; and finally, the market itself, considered as a social mechanism obliging all who participate in it to practice a sensible regard for others. . . . In actual practice, such [liberal] societies exhibit the most highly and complexly organized forms of life in all of human history.[12]

Novak's point here is well taken. We ought not let nostalgia for the small organic village impede our appreciation of the new forms of community when these new forms meet genuine human needs. At the same time, it seems to me too hasty to declare these communities to be a serious fulfillment of the Personalist objectives.

When Catholic Social Thought speaks about community in the fullest sense, it is not referring to what sociologists[13] have called "enclaves" which people form on the basis of their common needs, interests, and/or lifestyles. The important differences between many of these communities and community in the fuller sense is the element of commitment. Persons find fulfillment through joining communities not strictly on the basis of self-interest, but out of commitment to other persons within the community and also through the knowledge that the common good is also somehow served through joining. It has for example been a long and consistent teaching that workers join labor unions not only for self-interest, but on the basis of "solidarity" with other workers and precisely in order to contribute to the common good.[14]

If persons ultimately aspire to communion with one another, then enclaves which people form on the basis of their common needs, interests, and/or lifestyles are not the ideal and ought not dominate social life. The element of personal commitment in the sense of commitment of the members to one another as persons and commitment of the community to the wider common good is essential. The traditional structures of our families, neighborhoods, parishes, professional associations, town communities, civic organizations, and other associations have long included these two forms of commitment. The family for example is of course an important social ethical unit. Catholic Social Thought has long stressed the enduring nature of the commitment between members of a family, highlighting especially the life-long commitment of the spouses to each other. At the same time, the mutual commitment within the family is not to be closed and self-centered, but makes its own essential contributions to the life of the larger society.[15] The family is a witness for life through its prophetic mission in which conjugal love, fidelity, the training of children in love, hope, courage, faith, and justice are all indispensable to society. Analogously, we hope and expect that civic organizations of various types at the very least foster commitment to one another within their proper context. Finally, it is most certainly the case that professional organizations, such as those of nurses, lawyers, teachers, and doctors, are expected to work in solidarity not only for the mutual benefit of their members, but also to keep constantly the common good as a foremost consideration in all their activities and decisions.

Tragically, modern times have seen an erosion of this virtue of commitment in these traditional forms of social organizations. Divorce increasingly shatters marriages and wrecks what might have been a safe soil for the development of children. It has become increasingly common to hear the charge that the professions are no longer serving the common good as they ought. Our mobility as a culture, our tendency to work for the highest bidder, also results in severe dislocation and the weakening of our network of friendships. Membership in PTAs (parent teacher organizations) is reportedly at an all-time low. Personalism assigns responsibility less to the economic sector for these things than it does to the moral cultural sector which infuses social life with its own spirit. These weakenings of commitment have their roots not so much in economics as in a failure of the necessary educational and moral formation of the choosing agent.

The truth of this is perhaps most obvious in the case of marriage. I recall my own marriage instruction class within the Catholic Church some sixteen years ago, complete with a six-month waiting period before date of ceremony. Although at that point in my life I had never had a class in theology and submitted happily to the process, I harbored a number of critical questions about the process. A six-month waiting period seemed reasonable, and indeed it may prevent less serious couples from acting rashly. But the idea that the classes would assist somehow in reducing divorce rates by enabling participants to act more deliberately and rationally through preparation in the class and explanation about the true meaning of marriage clearly missed the mark. This was a triumph of the liberal anthropology (free, equal, rational) and the "fallacy of the rational solution" if ever I have heard it. I do not think people divorce for lack of anything supplied by such a class. People divorce these days because one or more parties lack a very particular set of character traits, skills, and attitudes which contribute to communal life and can only be formed over a lifetime through a very large battery of social opportunities made possible by communal life in the moral cultural sector. Only with such participation in these opportunities can one gain a sense of commitment to other participants and to the larger common good.

While these traditional societies are losing this sense of commitment, many of the new forms of social organization have done little to achieve it. Certainly the joint stock company, the corporation, the credit union, insurance and pension funds all contribute to society through their existence as well-run and profitable organizations. Well-run and profitable organizations must make efficient use of scarce resources while supplying products which consumers are willing and able to purchase. This is a part of good stewardship.They furthermore provide employment opportunities for persons to provide for themselves and their families, as well as offering opportunity for self-realization in the exercise of creativity and freedom at the workplace. So these organizations must already show a regard for the well being of others as a condition of their long-run profitability. It is of course possible to make a profit while failing to show consideration for the well being of others in different ways. The profit motive can also provide incentives for the degradation of the environment, employment practices that do not respect human dignity, greed and consumer fraud, and the betrayal of stockholder trust through abuses of managerial power. The two root expressions of selfish social attitudes and behaviors are the desire for material gain and for power.

The direction I would point to for the solution of these evils is admittedly a long-range one, and not a form of triage. The violence of increased government regulation will also find itself totally helpless to overcome every instance of these abuses which can only multiply exponentially among persons oriented exclusively toward profit and power. Personalism, recognizing the social nature of the human person, can only advocate the *renewal and transformation of communities which give character to persons and groups.* So I cannot offer a quick top-down solution which can be speedily executed through the fiat of social planners and the central government. This direction will, however, finally give attention to the long-run forces which tend to disintegrate the social fabric.

The renewal and transformation of communities comes about partially but not exclusively through voluntary actions in the moral cultural sector. The churches, civic organizations, and families should all reassert their own rights and especially responsibilities in these matters. Parents must once again parent in accordance with beliefs and values which they hold dear. In these days churches are increasingly retreating from playing a central role in American life. "The experts" in psychology, science, sociology, law, and education have in their own way marginalized religion to the enhancement of their own power and profit. Almost everywhere, groups must regain their sense of competence against the "experts."

The churches, of all institutions, ought to reassert their role in the formation of persons. How often have we all suffered sermons that seemed to be a mix of Thomas and Freud, with Freud receiving the lion's share of emphasis? The discussion and pursuit of value is an essential aspect to personal realization, and within religious traditions we do find discussion about and pursuit of what is ultimately real and valuable. Confidence in the human import of this theological discussion is essential. As is well known, the churches have a long, though spotted and imperfect, history of supporting the civil rights of oppressed and minority groups. Within the churches one can find both the will and the important intellectual resources to contribute to the common good through its expertise in humanity. Of all places, the bonds of community which enable human action in solidarity should be present in the churches. Michael Novak has, rightly in my judgment, advanced the following proposals:

> Give welfare benefits to young mothers of small children in congregant settings only (such as local churches or schools) in which they can be brought out of isolation and also learn how to care for children, how to study or work with others, and how to prepare themselves both for independent living and a potentially successful marriage.
>
> Turn every institution of civil society (including churches) to focus on the development of human capital in poor urban areas through the organization of academies, competitions, and skill oriented and habit developing training programs. Among others, churches, religious lay groups, the US military, auxiliary police forces, and sports associations—specialists in training young men—might run these programs. . . . Personally, I [Novak] recommend the Marianist or Christian Brothers of old: tough disciplinarians, motivated by unsentimental love.

Although Novak tends to stress the failure of the noneconomic sectors, my interest in practical reform will be different. Because the political, cultural, and economic sectors are mutually conditioning, optimally at least any significant reform strategy will actually help make the economic sector itself a contributing participant to good ethics.

An Integral Anthropology

Communitarianism is the first anthropological feature to be mentioned when discussing a Personalist Christian social anthropology. The second must be the understanding of the human person as body and spirit, an "incarnational" understanding of human makeup:

> Though made of body and soul, man is one. Through his bodily composition he gathers to himself the elements of the material world. Thus they reach their crown through him, and through him raise their voice in free praise of the creator.
>
> For this reason man is not allowed to despise his bodily life. Rather, he is obliged to regard his body as good and honorable since God created it and will raise it up on the last day.[16]

The assertion that bodily life is important is tantamount to saying that the material world and the "here and now" are also of critical concern for the Personalist perspective. There is no purely other worldly perspective to be found today in the social encyclicals if such ever were the case. Indeed, if salvation in the "hereafter" were the exclusive concern of the Church, there would be little need for the social encyclicals which have taken up the important issues of peace, justice, and liberation. Today Catholic Social Thought views action on behalf of justice as a "constitutive" dimension of the preaching of the Gospel.[17] The Church's mission of redemption and participation in building Christ's coming kingdom cannot be accomplished apart from the pursuit of justice.

Certainly basic material needs of flesh-and-blood individuals must be met as a condition for the possibility of human well being in all its aspects.[18] In the apostolic exhortation *Evangelii Nuntiandi* (1975), Pope Paul VI connects the idea of justice with evangelization. To speak of evangelization without speaking of justice in the political, economic, and cultural orders is to distort the concept. At the center of the Good News is the proclamation of liberation from *everything* that oppresses men and women.[19] The proclamation of the Gospel takes the human "person as the starting point" and affects humankind's criteria of "judgment, determining values, points of interest, lines of thought, sources of inspiration and models of life."[20] So this integral anthropology allows no significant area of human interest to fall outside of the concern of the Gospel, and it recognizes that these areas are linked in their impact on humankind. But this integral anthropology has implications for ethical method as well.

The implications of this integral anthropology stretch well beyond the duty of the Church, now commonly accepted within Christian theology, to concern itself with contemporary social issues. We are also pointed toward the more difficult task of conversation across disciplinary boundaries with the social sciences which in fact do not discuss the human person with the life of the spirit in mind. Indeed, the basic philosophical underpinnings of these tend to be materialist. But in this conversation, the Church and world discover together the truth about human persons:

> In order better to incarnate the one truth about man in different and constantly changing social, economic and political contexts, this teaching enters into dialogue with the various disciplines concerned with man. It assimilates what these disciplines have to contribute, and helps them to open themselves to a broader horizon, aimed at serving the individual person who is acknowledged and loved in the fullness of his or her vocation.[21]

Therefore, the moral theologian must pay careful attention not only to that data from theology which concerns the human person and his/her fulfillment, but also to the relevant sciences.

This mutually beneficial dialogue requires respect for the perspectives of the other partners. The social teachings have come to recognize the legitimate degree of autonomy to which these sciences are entitled for their proper functioning. Again and again Catholic Social Thought has admitted that it has no technical solutions by which the social sciences might be bypassed. Although the understandings of the human person on which the social sciences are based are admittedly only partial ones, they still advance our understanding toward the larger anthropological horizon. The greater threat to the dialogue in contemporary times is really the opposite one: the sciences about the human person (sociology, economics, education) no longer admit the need for a dialogue with theology. This is, I believe, not because of the much decried "secularism" of the modern world. Theology is hardly the only discipline which has become marginalized and shoved into the gutter of "private taste." The problem today lies rather in the supremacy in the areas of work and education given to technical reason and the refusal to engage in the sort of discussion about the human person to which theology, philosophy, poetry, art, and other disciplines might contribute. As David Tracy has concluded, "where art is marginalized, religion is privatized."[22]

Theology, art, and poetry are marginalized since these are relegated to the realm of "individual taste" and thereby made impotent as resources for discussion about the content of and methods of achieving the common good. The vacuum is readily filled by the high priests from science, departments of education, economics, and from all those areas of research which claim specialized technical knowledge. It is not surprising that competent authorities in these various areas exercise some imperialism when the opportunity presents itself through our retreat within the moral cultural sector. It is not the existence of scientific inquiry and the existence of experts which is per se a problem:

> Scientific inquiry does not necessitate dominance, mastery, control; it bears within itself its own immanent norms of critical, emancipatory self-transcendence opening it to values, ethics, art, religion, to the fundamental questions. . . . Technology need not prove technocracy.[23]

Nevertheless, when this imperialism is exercised, the result is an unwelcome tyranny over persons, their communities, and nature. The spiritual aspirations of the human person go unrecognized. Economics becomes a purely technical science guided by purely utilitarian goals that no longer receive examination. Education can become oriented to the achievement of behavioral "outcomes" in students which form the child only as a potential economic agent (worker and consumer) but neglect the liberal course of study. Sociology can become a means for social manipulation without evaluation of the ends for which this expertise is being used and without regard to the observance of human rights in the process.

How else can the often repeated phrase "trust the experts" function in our time except to reinforce the views, interests, and prestige of those who stand to gain through the imperialism of technical reason. The danger to the full development of the human person is further clarified when we consider that these areas of scientific inquiry are materialist in their basic method. For Christian Personalism, progress is never identified purely with the advancement of technical reason. Genuine progress must somehow advance the causes of persons as persons who have spiritual aspirations.

Personal Existence: Finitude and Sin

A third and related factor in a Christian Personalist anthropology concerns the limitations imposed by human finitude and also sin. While theology points to transcendence and to the more profound aspirations of humankind, the sciences remind us of the limitations of human existence. They reveal the substructures that give definition to human existence and at the same time limit its possibilities. Matter is not spirit, and a sober realism about human possibilities must be a part of any ethic. That is, there are many limitations, also technical limitations, and not only moral problems that must be overcome as humankind moves forward to a Personalist future. The Kingdom of God is not realized solely through good intentions, nor quickly, nor apart from human participation and the growth of knowledge and wisdom.

Furthermore, theology remains acutely and painfully aware of human fallenness. Sin, as an egoism which separates us from God, ourselves, and others, is continuously operative.[24] For Catholic Social Thought, sin is rooted in the individual actions of persons who misuse their freedom. These sinful actions influence social structures so much so that they leave a permanent impression on our institutions and practices. The two root expressions of selfish social attitudes and behaviors are the desire for material gain and the desire for power.

These two are "indissolubly united" in the modern world.[25] We encounter these two when we observe a corporation which gains influence in an area or foreign country and conducts business without regard for the social fabric or ecological systems. We encounter structural and personal sin equally as clearly when we observe a public-sector bureaucracy with political power which is exercised for the financial gain of the bureaucracy itself and not for the common good.

Besides the fact that sin has individual and collective dimensions, sin has a third characteristic which is equally important. Individual and collective sin is tenacious; from the "dawn of history"[26] humankind has misused its freedom and set back true human fulfillment. Personalism seeks to diminish this tendency toward sin but realizes that its complete elimination is not a possibility in the present time. Therefore, systems must be designed that draw out the maximum amount of justice in a given situation. On this point we see development within the social teachings.

In light of the Great Depression, *Quadragesimo Anno* (Pius XI, 1931) had called for massive structural changes in Western political economics along the lines of corporatism. Corporatism was a conception of society as an hierarchically ordered harmony organized for the common good according to vocational groups and not classes. The expectation was that the political and economic sectors would cooperate for the common good as would the vocational groups within the economic sector. The idea has long since been abandoned[27] because the teachings have come to a greater appreciation of the ways in which liberal systems of political economy work to bring out justice in the face of human egoism. Corporative systems of political economy give insufficient attention to the reality of our fallen condition. Such systems largely ignore issues of power and conflict of interest, precisely the two defining aspects of sin which the documents since the Second Vatican Council understand to be "indissolubly united" in the modern world. Today, Catholic Social Thought has abandoned corporatist models and has also come to an acceptance of market competition in the context of an appropriate political and social framework:[28]

In one passage of *Rerum Novarum* he [Leo XIII] presents the organization of society according to the three powers—legislative, executive and judicial—something which at the time represented a novelty in Church teaching. Such an ordering reflects a realistic vision of man's social nature, which calls for legislation capable of protecting the freedom of all. To that end, it is preferable that each power be balanced by other powers and by other spheres of responsibility which keep it within proper bounds. This is the principle of the "rule of law.". . . authentic democracy is possible only in a state ruled by law, and on the basis of a correct conception of the human person.

The achievement of balances in power is a genius of liberal institutions. Therefore, considerations of human finitude and sin will move Christian Personalists to an appreciation of liberal political-economic systems and to an understanding of the protests of economists and social scientists who at times must point out that the "best is enemy to the good."

Human Agency: Creativity and Freedom

Freedom attains its full development only by accepting the truth.[29]

The understanding of liberty here differs from our liberal authors of chapter 2 in two important ways: First, Personalism understands liberty to be oriented to authentic value and, second, liberty receives form in the context of a community with others. We find ourselves as members of families, neighborhoods, churches, professional associations, town communities, civic organizations, and other associations which constitute the opportunities for the proper exercise of human freedom. What Personalism laments with the growth of the state and large bureaucracies is not the loss of the abstract liberal "individual freedom" but the loss of freedom and responsibility which is exercised by persons in community with others.

The Personalist understanding of liberty is unlike that of the libertarian Robert Nozick. Liberty has a right and a wrong exercise since it exists to empower persons in their pursuit of value:

Only in freedom can man direct himself toward goodness. Our contemporaries make much of this freedom and pursue it eagerly;

and rightly so, to be sure. Often, however, they foster it perversely as a license for doing whatever pleases them, even if it is evil.

For its part, authentic freedom is an exception sign of the divine image within man. For God has willed that man be left "in the hand of his own counsel" so that he can seek his Creator spontaneously, and come freely to utter and blissful perfection through loyalty to him. Hence man's dignity demands that he act according to a knowing and free choice. Such a choice is personally motivated and prompted from within. It does not result from blind internal impulse nor from mere external pressure.[30]

If, as Thomas says, the law is training in virtue, then certainly laws ought to exist against those activities which hinder the formation of virtue. Of course, Thomas also says that laws can only restrain the greater vices, and this remains true today for a number of practical and epistemological reasons. The problem is not primarily a political failure in which the arm of the law requires greater exercise, nor is it a failure of the economic sector which makes many goods and services available. It is a failure of the moral cultural sector which has ceased to exercise its proper role in the formation of the choosing agent as it once did. This is precisely the position of John Paul II for whom the excess of consumerism have their roots, not so much in economics as in a failure of the necessary educational and moral formation of the choosing agent.[31]

When freedom is correctly understood, "it is not the power to be able to do this or that, but the power to decide about oneself and to actualize oneself."[32] Therefore, freedom must be oriented toward and at the service of authentically human values. The moral formation of the choosing agent lies at the beginning and end of any exercise of personal freedom. Our own prior formation helps direct any free action, and at the same time this action leaves its own imprint on personality. A society such as ours which accords to individuals such extraordinary possibilities for free action offers immense opportunity for self-actualization, but it also offers immense opportunity for self-disintegration and depersonalization.

The abuse of this freedom, and the consequent personal disintegration, occurs today to such an extent that we have certainly become numb to the lesser abuses while the larger abuses are the central issues of public policy. Through the staggering number of hours spent watching inane television, through consumerism and the endless pursuit of trivial commodities, through the use of mind-altering drugs, through the availability of pornography, American society is in danger of being swept up in a tidal wave of complete triviality and personal disintegration. Of course, those who seek to remedy these and other such activities through the coercive power of the law understand neither the practical nor epistemological problems with doing so, nor are they adequately focused on the central role played by the choosing agent. Solutions appropriate to free and creative persons must optimally aim to form persons who choose authentic self-actualization. This can only occur in community with others in which persons receive their formation and in which commitment to authentic values is kept alive. These communities, be they families, churches, civic and/or professional associations, will require the courage to assert themselves against the "experts" and against outside forces which threaten their integrity and commitment to human values.

A person's pursuit of value should take place in work life if time spent doing work is not to be totally alienating. We choose jobs and careers according to the interests and deeper values which we hold. The development of a full theory of value is not possible here, nor is it advisable given the pluralism in individual vocation. However, I do wish to point out that personal development is advanced largely through one's vocation or work. Work is a good thing for our humanity since "through work man not only transforms nature, adapting it to his own needs, but he also achieves fulfillment as a human being and indeed in a sense becomes 'more a human being.' "[33]

Work has not only the commonly recognized objective or technical significance as the means by which goods and services are produced. Work has a deep subjective meaning as well. When persons fulfill the vocation proper to them, they make family and social life possible by supplying the necessary goods and services, and they participate in and contribute to a growing social heritage. Furthermore, this enables families and societies to attain their proper ends, especially the proper development and formation of persons. Through work persons, families, and societies advance the process of "becoming a human being."[34]

So the importance of personal vocation as an expression of personal freedom and creativity can hardly be overstated.[35] We expect that any attempts to assist individuals in their condition that do not lead them to work and the fulfillment of a vocation will be inadequate from a moral (and not just an economic) perspective. Furthermore, any attempts to assist individuals which do not nourish the life of the social structures, including families, civic organizations, local churches, and other community-based organizations, must also be identified as morally inadequate. Because we take the moral order seriously, we do not expect such attempts to succeed economically in the long run. These in a nutshell are the most important reasons why we must pronounce the "first compromise" (described in chapter 2) as dead. A new understanding from the moral perspective must scrutinize a system of political economy for its social anthropology; its understanding of human freedom, creativity, finitude, and sin; as well as our social nature and our nature as body and soul.

Equality

The issue of equality is a difficult one to discuss in modern liberal society first of all because the trained mind cannot possibly concur with the popular notions which surround it, and because this failure to concur inevitably subjects one to charges of elitism or even worse. However, Christian Personalism must draw careful distinctions about what equality can and cannot mean; I concur with the Catholic Personalist philosopher Gabriel Marcel who says:

> Nothing could be more deceptive than the formulations with which the great men of the French Revolution allowed themselves to be satisfied. They believed that liberty, equality, and fraternity could all be placed on the same level. I hope we shall be able to recognize that equality has to do with the abstract; that it is not men who are equal, for men are not triangles or quadrilaterals. What are equal, what must be postulated as equal, are not human beings but rights and duties which men must reciprocally recognize.[36]

Catholic Social Thought is not given to this false spirit of abstraction. Catholic Social Thought recognizes the different gifts and indeed callings which persons have, and consequentially, it recognizes the varied ways in which persons and groups relate to one another in civil society. When it claims that "there is a basic equality between all men and it must be given ever greater recognition,"[37] it speaks about certain basic rights and duties.

To be sure, Catholic Social Thought has come to a greater appreciation of the sense in which "equality" must be predicated on human beings. This has in large part happened not only through reflection on the Gospel, but also through cross-fertilization with *liberal* theory and practice. Catholic Social Thought emerges from a theological tradition very much at home with a hierarchical worldview. Within the institutional Church, the proper order of relations has been a rule by priests in which the pope, bishops, priests, deacons, and, lastly, lay persons exercise their ordered rights and responsibilities. Early Catholic Social Thought understood the political world from a similar perspective. It stressed the rights and responsibilities of public authorities in achieving the common good and discouraged more active and forceful displays of labor power including strikes.[38] Indeed, until the Second Vatican Council, the rights and responsibilities of public authorities in achieving the common good included favoring the "true" religion. It was only in the document *Dignitatis Humanae* that the concept of religious liberty was more adequately developed according to moral insights taken from liberal democracies.[39]

On economic matters, basic human equality has received a stronger and also increasing emphasis within Catholic Social Thought. The basic equality among persons has been the basis for the call to provide all persons, and especially the least advantaged, with the necessary material and nonmaterial support to achieve the ends of human life. The teachings have never called for complete egalitarianism; there is no moral basis for a call that all persons should be equal in matters of income or wealth. There is, however, a strong insistence that our basic dignity requires the meeting of basic economic rights. Therefore, Catholic Social Thought is inconsistent with radical egalitarianism but does endorse a much more moderate goal aimed at meeting what may be called minimum human economic rights.

Personalist Method

The most salient feature of the Personalist method of Catholic Social Thought is its "engagement" with the existing human situation. With the development of a Personalist perspective, Catholic Social Thought has paid increasing attention to the "signs of the times" in its social ethical method. In *Gaudium et Spes* (par. 4),

> Since the Church lives in history, she ought to "scrutinize the signs of the times" and interpret them in the light of the Gospel. Sharing the noblest aspirations of men and suffering when she sees them not satisfied, she wishes to help them attain their full flowering, and that is why she offers men what she possesses as her characteristic attribute: a global vision of man and of the human race.[40]

Precisely because personal existence is historical existence, attention must be paid to the "signs of the times." According to John Paul II, work is the key to the social question today. Women and men were created in the image of God through the mandate to subdue the earth. Work here receives a broad definition as any authentic labor which leads to personal development. It is the world of work in which the person freely pursues a vocation, so we look here for a reading of the signs of the times.

Christian Personalism will draw on insights from the properly theological sources, including the Scriptures, the liturgy, and the tradition broadly understood. But the moralist who works within a Christian Personalist method will also draw from the insights of economics, psychology, sociology, philosophy, and other sources of moral insight within culture. Attention to these sources are necessary if the human condition and the signs of the times are to be adequately understood. The important task is to reinterpret the more properly theological sources in light of new questions and in light of new insights.

The Christian Scriptures certainly speak much about economic justice in the context of the agricultural economies of the time. An entire basic ethical perspective along with a corresponding constellation of ethical principles and norms are developed which presume an agricultural setting. The size and quality of the harvest is largely not within human power to control. An agricultural society is essentially a zero-sum society in which any gain for one person represents an equal loss for another. Giving thanks to the Lord for one's provisions must not be understood as a simple metaphysical affirmation that the

Lord is somehow the ultimate provider, but it expresses a real experience of powerlessness in doing much about the size of the harvest which can therefore only be received as a gift from the Lord.[41] Of course, if provisions are received like manna from heaven, there are no prior ownership rights (Nozick) and the central question will be one of distribution. Furthermore, riches on the part of one party *necessarily* imply poverty on the part of another. The parties exist potentially in the relationship of oppressor and oppressed. The proclamation of justice to one party must be a declaration of woe to the other. This basic perspective accounts for much of the emphasis on "distributive justice" found in biblical and liberation ethics today.

Christian Personalism today cannot be satisfied with a hegemony of this manna-from-heaven approach to economic issues. Modern economies are not agriculturally based, and modern economies are certainly not zero-sum economies. Riches on the part of one party need not imply poverty on the part of any other party. As was demonstrated in chapter 1, the economic pie has grown radically since the advent of capitalism. Therefore, a contemporary ethical method must pay attention to economic science, to a proper view of human agency, and to the priority of labor over capital. Still, Scripture remains an essential source as it illuminates a basic perspective and theological anthropology; there is no *Christian* Personsalism without it. However, the longevity and usefulness of certain methods, principles, and especially concrete norms must continuously be reexamined.

The primary concern of the Personalist is the "priority of labor over capital." Labor receives a broad definition; it is not restricted to a Marxist understanding which associates it with a distinct propertyless class. Similarly, the definition of capital for John Paul includes "not only the natural resources placed at man's disposal, but also the whole collection of means by which man appropriates natural resources and transforms them in accordance with his needs."[42] Capital then includes the entire system of physical things and human practices set in motion in the production process. Capital in this sense has no other purpose than to serve authentically human purposes.

The signs of the times must be read to determine the extent to which capital does serve labor. Careful social scientific work is necessary for this descriptive task. There is then a mutually beneficial dialogue at all levels, those of basic perspective and practical application, between

Christian social ethics and the various disciplines which claim knowledge about the human person.[43]

This dialogue should not be seen as an abstract dialogue only among experts in the various fields. The dialogue must occur primarily through the actual involvement of the Church in the world. The Church with its traditional and well-known official apolitical stance represents a somewhat inconsistent Personalist method. For Mounier, deductive and crudely empirical ethical methods are only overcome through engagement in historical movements of personalization. Engagement in concrete historical movements makes it possible to transcend the dichotomy, not by means of a middle way between the two, which is also an abstraction, but by shedding unique light on the dichotomy:

> Abstention has a habit of adopting neither-neither attitudes. Others prefer a mathematical position such as (a + b)/2 which they claim to be the very reverse of utopianism, but which is really a rather special version, the middle of the road. The method is highly elaborate, and consists of separating a complex reality into two extremes, in order to afford oneself the satisfaction of assuming that reason and good sense are an equal distance from either. This is really an eclectic abstraction favored by the habitual liking for *immobility*.[44]

Mounier's incarnational perspective resolves the question only through involvement in historical movements consistent with personalization. Following Mounier, I suggest that greater involvement and engagement on the part of the Church in causes for justice might be entirely appropriate from a Personalist perspective. Contemporary authors from very different perspectives have said as much about Catholic Social Thought.

Donal Dorr, writing from a socialist orientation, argues that the core demand of justice today is organized around an "option for the poor." This option for the poor is almost definitionally a commitment to support radical transformation of the structures of society in order to establish an alternative to the capitalist or free enterprise model. Dorr believes that the Church must practice what it proclaims:

> The option for the poor requires . . . a commitment by Church leaders not to collude with oppressive regimes but to campaign

actively for structural justice in society and to take the risk of throwing the authority of the official Church behind efforts to resist oppression and exploitation.[45]

An abstract commitment to certain ideals is not enough. The Church must be truly engaged in the world as theory and practice mutually illuminate one another.

Richard John Neuhaus, writing from a very different basic perspective, agrees with Dorr on the need for concrete engagement. Neuhaus, editor of *First Things* and the author of a number of widely read works, including *The Naked Public Square* and *The Catholic Moment,* argues that it is time to develop a spirituality of economic enterprise.[46] Consistent with his earlier works, Neuhaus argues that the Judeo-Christian tradition provides the meaning system and the plausibility structure for moral discourse in America. The American Puritan-Lockean synthesis is sustained with warrants from this tradition. Given the unwillingness of liberal "mainline-oldline" Protestantism to perform this function, Neuhaus looks to Catholic social teaching and especially to *Centesimus Annus.* Catholic social teaching contains public arguments that propose "a fresh way of thinking about modernity and about democracy in the public order" for those who enter into conversation with it and engage it seriously. The most worthy contributors to this discussion speak of real-world correlates to their theories.

Personalist Interpretation of Social Justice

For a Personalist ethic, the personal universe gives definition to the moral universe. Action directed toward *Personalist goals* and fully "engaged" in the world is integral to the moral life. Since *Quadragesimo Anno* the documents of Catholic Social Thought have used the term "social justice" to give direction to this social action.

To my mind, Michael Novak has done much to recover an unmuddled interpretation of the term "social justice."[47] This modern term originates within Catholic Social Thought in *Quadragesimo Anno* (1931) by Pius XI. In light of the Great Depression, in *Quadragesimo Anno* Pius XI had called for massive structural changes in Western political economies along the lines of corporatism. The intention was to offer in a new term a substantive understanding of justice suitable for the rapid changes which characterize the modern age.

Writers have treated "social justice" not as a personal virtue, but as a preferred principle of social organization (this is also precisely what John Rawls does when he describes justice as the first virtue of institutions). For most modern interpreters of *Quadragesimo Anno* who write with the betterment of the welfare state in mind, realizing the principle usually includes first enlarging and then harnessing the power of the state. Novak correctly complains that to advocate social justice as a principle is to advocate one particular social order, and to "prejudice arguments concerning means and ends by defining opponents as 'unjust.' "[48]

For Novak, social justice is not an ideologically bound principle of social organization but "a specific modern form of the ancient virtue of justice" which is exercised when persons join voluntarily with others to bring about social change for the common good. Given the modern recognition that the common good is only achieved with the cooperation of persons who join in free associations, this virtue need not be the sole possession of those who favor enlarging the central authority. For Novak, the common good emerges in a "spontaneous" way through the free choices of persons. This modern conception leaves open the nature of the common good and it certainly leaves open the means to achieve it.

For Novak, medieval societies operated on a less complex notion of social justice and the common good than do advanced societies. Medieval societies operated on an epistematic assumption that officers of the state knew the common good better than others and were inclined to pursue it. The fact that neither of these claims would receive widespread acceptance today is a deeper justification for the modern emphasis on democratic rule and systems of checks and balances. Therefore, Novak takes a firm stance against a deductive approach at central planning. Today the common good emerges spontaneously and, from any particular point of view, through contrary purposes. Although no one takes direct aim at achieving the common good, no one actually intends it, it is nevertheless achieved according to Novak through a manner described by Friedrich von Hayek as "catallaxy,"[49] through voluntary exchange and cooperation in pursuit of self-interest.

Novak offers a brief analogy with marriage which helps make his concept of the common good more clear. In marriage both spouses will their common good in a formal sense, but the two can never know materially what shape this common good might take. They express "good will" toward one another, but cannot actually map out a plan describing the concrete shape of their joint life. Therefore, they take each other "for better or worse." The common good of society is much like this; citizens only will the common good formally while acting in a culture of pluralism with different "intentions, aims, and purposes."[50] The desire to share common intentions, aims, and purposes is a nostalgia for tribal solidarities. It was this nostalgia that Adolf Hitler traded upon as have all modern collectivists.[51]

I do not wish unnecessarily to exaggerate my differences with Novak, since I agree with the core insight that social justice ought not be seen as a *static principle* of social organization. I also agree quite strongly that the achievement of the common good will involve the expansion of civil society and the contraction of centralized political authority. However, Novak's reluctance to offer a more substantive vision of the common good is very problematic because the processes and outcomes of collective behavior will lack a well-grounded normative yardstick. Structural criticism and reform are more difficult to make both theoretically and practically. I do not agree that the common good will necessarily be achieved through the free choices and contrary purposes of individuals. Free persons must step forward and assume collective responsibility for the final shape of the structures which they bring into being. This will involve observation, criticism, and visionary action guiding the system as a whole. One does not necessarily speak of implementing a "draconian scheme"[52] when one says that a (Personalist) vision can be systematically advanced using the powers of the state to enable civil society and to *guide* movement toward (not implementation of) a vision. Modern interpreters of Catholic Social Thought have surely fallen into some overemphasis on the rights and responsibilities of the state. The state must be subservient to civil society,[53] but it seems unwise to ignore the repeated assertions within Catholic Social Thought about the need for a central authority that does enable, guide, and correct course as necessary.

It seems to me that Neuhaus[54] has made a related criticism of Novak although less from an ethical perspective and more from a sociological one. Neuhaus, decrying the "naked public square" in which religion and religiously-grounded values are excluded from American public life, cannot agree with Novak that a democratic society is marked by a "reverential emptiness" at the heart of the public order. The sociological meaning of this is the naked public square which leaves public life unaccountable to moral resources. For Neuhaus, it is actually within the Judeo-Christian tradition that democracy and democratic rights find their ground and protection. Neuhaus does not speak of coercion or imposition of this tradition, but only of reasoned discourse and persuasion. What I have pointed out here is the ethical dimension of this problem in Novak's perspective.

Evil enters in where capital does not serve labor, but instead labor surrenders to impersonal systems which enslave it for the advancement of the power and profit of some particular interest. Therefore, persons who wish to practice and develop the virtue of social justice will cooperate with others in actions which aim to establish the priority of persons over the processes and bureaucracies which enslave them. This applies when we speak of an oversized "social assistance state" which deprives people of their legitimate sphere of action; of traditional welfare programs which create dependency and promote behavior which is counterproductive from a social and from an individual perspective; of corporations which treat persons as assets to be hired and dismissed casually, or exploited in other ways; of nations in which foreign policy is driven solely by economic interests without regard for the culture and needs in other lands; or of a distribution of income which disrupts the social fabric and offends the dignity of all and especially of the least advantaged.

Positively, establishing the priority of persons over the processes and bureaucracies which enslave them involves constant attention in the formation of social policy to those truths which concern our sociality, our existence as incarnate beings, the reality of finitude and sin, and our drive toward freedom and creativity. According to Catholic Social Thought, today this will involve an emphasis on building up civil society so that all persons may exercise their creativity and freedom. It will involve some activity and legislation by the state aimed at bringing all persons "into the cycle of exchange and productivity;"[55] only this can be a genuine option for the poor.

We look for the engagement and involvement in concrete experiences and problems of our time in the manner spoken about by Dorr and Neuhaus as we chart a course toward a more Personalist future. But we must chart this course between the Charybdis and Scylla of utopianism and cynicism. Neither utopianism nor cynicism shows sufficient understanding for our nature as finite and sinful beings who nevertheless strive for genuine fulfillment.

Conclusion

Following Mounier, we have discussed the Personalism of Catholic Social Thought in the categories of *perspective, method, and exigency.* Throughout, we have found place for contemporary liberal notions of freedom, equality, and rationality, while modifying and also supplementing them with our social anthropology. The central task of an economic system is always to meet human needs and at the same time to provide for the development of human subjects. From the moral and practical perspectives, these two cannot be separated, and they are achieved simultaneously or not at all. Therefore, we have put a sound anthropology which is supported by Catholic Social Thought at the center of our social ethical perspective. In the next chapter, we move to a discussion of practice which coheres with the perspective developed in this chapter.

Notes

1. Michael Novak makes this quite clear and, correctly I think, criticizes those who misunderstand his work as libertarian. See: Michael Novak, *The Catholic Ethic and the Spirit of Capitalism* (New York: Free Press, 1993), p.137.
2. Emmanuel Mounier, *Personalism* (Notre Dame, Indiana: University of Notre Dame Press, 1950).
3. Emmanuel Mounier, *Be Not Afraid: A Denunciation of Despair* (New York: Sheed and Ward, 1946), p.193.
4. Mounier, *Personalism*, p.17.
5. *Gaudium et Spes,* par. 12.
6. "Gaudium et Spes," in *Vatican Council II: The Conciliar and Post Conciliar Documents,* general editor, Austin Flannery, O.P., (Collegeville, Minnesota: The Liturgical Press, 1979), par. 12.

7. "Gaudium et Spes," in *Vatican Council II: The Conciliar and Post Conciliar Document,* par. 17.
8. Michael J. Schuck, *That They Be One: The Social Teaching of the Papal Encyclicals 1740–1989* (Washington, D.C.: Georgetown University Press, 1991), p.180.
9. Schuck, *That They Be One,* p.180.
10. Schuck, *That They Be One,* p.180.
11. *Gaudium et Spes,* par. 13.
12. Novak, *The Catholic Ethic,* p.27.
13. Robert Bellah, et al., *Habits of the Heart: Individualism and Commitment in American Life* (New York: Harper & Row, 1985), p.72.
14. See: Leo XIII, *Rerum Novarum,* par. 36f.; and John Paul II, *Laborem Exercens,* par. 8.
15. United States Catholic Bishops, *Human Life in Our Day,* par. 15f.
16. *Gaudium et Spes,* par. 14.
17. *Justice in the World,* (Synod of Bishops, 1971), introduction.
18. This integral anthropology brings to light the different senses in which persons find their fulfillment. John Finnis, for example, has specified seven basic aspects of human well-being which should be promoted by any just social order: life, knowledge, play, aesthetic experience, sociability, practical reasonableness, and religion. For Finnis, "the basic human goods, or values, are not mere abstractions; they are aspects—all the constitutive aspects—of the being and well-being of flesh and blood individuals. They are aspects of human personality." Although I find Finnis's explication of basic values illustrative and not incorrect and would offer them to the reader who has no better list, for our purposes agreement need not be demanded on an exhaustive statement about what is substantively required by our integral anthropology in terms of human well-being. Catholic Social Thought certainly claims no knowledge of an exhaustive list. Once again, by the central affirmation of free and creative persons, the spirit of Personalism leads to caution when listing such items. See: John Finnis, *Natural Law and Natural Rights* (Oxford: Clarendon Press, 1980), pp.86–90.
19. *Evangelii Nuntiandi,* par. 9.
20. *Evangelii Nuntiandi,* par. 19.
21. *Centesimus Annus,* par. 59.
22. David Tracy, *The Analogical Imagination: Christian Theology and the Culture of Pluralism* (New York: Crossroad, 1986), p.13.
23. Tracy, *The Analogical Imagination: Christian Theology and the Culture of Pluralism,* pp.353–4.
24. *Gaudium et Spes,* par. 37.

25. *Sollicitudo Rei Socialis,* par. 37.

26. *Gaudium et Spes,* par. 13.

27. Personalist thinkers who anticipated the turn toward Personalism of the Second Vatican Council reached this position sooner. According to Mounier:

> Some thinkers imagine a *corporative* economy modeled upon the human organism, and postulate a harmony of workers, employers, nation and state by a mythical analogy which is in striking contradiction with the actual and enduring divergences of interests. (*Personalism,* p.105)

28. John Paul II, *Centesimus Annus,* par. 44f.

29. *Centesimus Annus,* par. 46.

30. *Gaudium et Spes,* par. 17.

31. *Centesimus Annus,* par. 36.

32. Karl Rahner, *Foundations of Christian Faith: An Introduction to the Idea of Christianity* (New York: Crossroad, 1987), p.38.

33. John Paul II, *Laborem Exercens,* par. 9.

34. John Paul II, *Laborem Exercens,* par. 10.

35. Emmanuel Mounier also saw the essential connection between freedom, vocation, and value:

> A person is a spiritual being, constituted as such by its manner of existence and independence of being; it maintains this existence by its adhesion to a hierarchy of values that it has freely adopted, assimilated, and lived by its own responsible activity and by a constant interior development; thus it unifies all its activity in freedom and by means of creative acts develops the individuality of its vocation. (*A Personalist Manifesto* [New York: Longmans, Green and Co., 1938] p.68).

36. Gabriel Marcel, *Man Against Mass Society* (South Bend, Indiana: Gateway Editions, Ltd., 1978), p.161.

37. *Gaudium et Spes,* par. 17.

38. Leo XIII, *Rerum Novarum,* par. 40.

39. It was, of course, the American Jesuit, John Courtney Murray, whose work in the journal *Theological Studies* and later at the council helped move Catholic Social Thought forward on this matter.

40. *Gaudium et Spes,* par. 4.

41. Deuteronomy 8:18.

42. John Paul II, *Laborem Exercens,* par. 12.

43. Mounier certainly agreed with this need for interdisciplinary dialogue. An important implication of historical and embodied existence combined with the movement toward personalization is the impotency of abstract idealist and abstract materialist doctrines. Idealist doctrines are

impotent since they neglect biological and economic necessities, while materialist doctrines are impotent for the opposite reason.

> In every practical problem, the solution must be verified at the level of the biological and economic substructures, if the measures proposed for higher reasons are to be viable. . . . Reciprocally, the biological or economic solution of a human problem, closely though it may conform to elementary needs, will be imperfect and precarious if it does not take account of the profounder aspirations of man. (*Personalism*, p.2)

44. Mounier, *Be Not Afraid*, pp.128–9.
45. Donal Dorr, *Option for the Poor: A Hundred Years of Catholic Social Teaching*, second edition (Maryknoll, New York: Orbis Press, 1992), p.2.
46. Richard John Neuhaus, *Doing Well and Doing Good: The Challenge to the Christian Capitalist* (New York: Doubleday, 1992).
47. Novak, *The Catholic Ethic and the Spirit of Capitalism*, ch. 3.
48. Novak, *The Catholic Ethic and the Spirit of Capitalism*, p.77.
49. Novak, *The Catholic Ethic and the Spirit of Capitalism*, pp.81–2.
50. Michael Novak, *Free Persons and the Common Good* (New York: Madison Books, 1989), p.83.
51. Novak, *Free Persons and the Common Good*, p.84.
52. Novak, *The Catholic Ethic and the Spirit of Capitalism*, p.85.
53. *Quadragesimo Anno*, par. 49.
54. Richard John Neuhaus, *The Naked Public Square* (Grand Rapids, Michigan: William B. Eerdmans Publishing Co., 1984), p.121.
55. Neuhaus, *Doing Well and Doing Good*, p.211.

III

TOWARD A CHRISTIAN CAPITALISM

5

Christian Personalism: Toward Implementation

Christians working to bring about that "civilization of love" which will include the entire ethical and social heritage of the Gospel are today faced with an unprecedented challenge. This task calls for renewed reflection on what constitutes the relationship between the supreme commandment of love and the social order considered in all its complexity. —Congregation for the Doctrine of the Faith

"Neither Christian ethicists nor bishops nor the church as a whole are [*sic*] in a position to create employment by fiat. . . . The task, then, is to move beyond moral proclamation to careful analysis of modes of implementing the right to employment. Concern with implementation is itself a genuinely moral concern, not simply a technical or political one.[1]" "*The real problem of social morality is to integrate various aspects of personal well being into "reasonable commitments, projects, and actions that go to make up one or other of the many admirable forms of human life."*[2]

There are a number of real-world efforts surfacing which I think constitute such examples of reasonable projects. One particularly impressive initiative which was uncovered in my research is Workforce America, currently operating in Harlem. Philosophically, the intention of the organization is to raise the personal capital of those otherwise qualified adults who are trapped in low-paying jobs and move them into the professional ranks. Workforce America is the not-for-profit arm of the Five O'Clock Club.[3] Kate Wendleton, president of The Five O'Clock Club, a national career counseling organization, and founder of Workforce America explains it this way:

> Workforce America is the bridge from jobs to careers for inner-city adults. We're taking those in low paying, dead-end jobs and facilitating their entry into professional careers with futures, thus helping to close the great economic divide in America. This is not a "welfare to work" program. . . . Half of our clients are already working, but we stay with them for eight to ten years and help them solidly move up the ranks. For example, clerks from Barnes & Noble with university degrees move into serious career tracks. *Every* person in the program goes through a process to discover his or her life vision and then works towards that.
>
> Workforce America is a process of social support: members give and receive help from others in the immediate group, those already well networked in the professional labor force, those in other Five O'Clock Clubs, as well as highly qualified career counselors. Members often bring their friends into the group.
>
> We have proven methods and have achieved a significant amount of success. However, we could use funding to expand this program into other cities such as South Central L.A., Detroit, and other obvious choices. We prefer corporate and not government funding because our methods are innovative—and correct—and do not fit into the usual government benchmark of simply getting a person a job, any job. We are trying to address the serious, long-term problem of moving people into good, productive, personally satisfying careers.

So, I do think that there are already such reasonable and promising projects which are consistent with the ethical theory laid out in this book, but which unfortunately cannot all be addressed in detail here. I want to focus now on a very broad and ambitious economywide reform not currently implemented.

In this chapter, one practical area of interest will be addressed using the ethical theory developed in the previous chapters. I will discuss the so called "share economy." There are of course those who will insist that it is theology's business to be prophetic, critical, and to denounce injustice. These things are doubtless true. But from a Personalist perspective, prophecy, criticism, and denunciation without serious technical understanding of the problem and subject matter, and without some attempt to "reconstruct," amounts to little more than nonsense and background noise and is very embarrassing to those who believe that the audience for systematic theology (and especially moral theology) includes not only the Church, but also society and the academy.

The common good will be achieved not only through the free choices and contrary purposes of individuals, but only when free persons assume responsibility collectively for the final shape of the structures which they bring into being. Persons with the virtue of social justice must step forward and assume collective and individual responsibility for the structures in which they participate. Therefore, persons who wish to practice and develop the virtue of social justice will cooperate with others in actions which aim to achieve the common good, understood as the priority of persons over the bureaucracies and processes in which they participate.

The common good has received the following, now classic yet formal, definition in Catholic Social Thought

> This [the common good] embraces the sum total of those conditions of social living, whereby men are enabled more fully and more readily to achieve their own perfection.[4]

So at this point we must give whatever specification possible to those actions and projects which promote the common good in the context of American society. We draw on the Christian Personalist social anthropology of chapter 4 in which the liberal anthropology of free, rational, and equal was greatly expanded to give emphasis to: human social nature, human existence as body and spirit, human participation in sin, creativity and freedom, and a proper understanding of our basic equality.

Methodologically, we must continue to pay careful attention to the signs of the times, to use insights from the social sciences, and to commit ourselves to addressing and engaging the concrete situation of American capitalism.

In what follows of this chapter, I present an illustrative reform agenda to accompany the moral perspective developed up to this point. I argue that the "share economy" shows an appreciation of the social nature of the human person and advances solidarity among workers as they share a common fate. It promises to help meet human bodily and material needs since it promises greater micro- and macroeconomic efficiency. As creative and free human subjects, workers experience more stable employment and greater participation in profit sharing and decision making; alienation is thereby reduced. The basic commitment to full employment is required by our concept of equal basic human rights; all persons are entitled to the necessary social conditions for the possibility of their own flourishing. The share economy successfully moves past and around the older Keynesian agenda. Furthermore, the importance of decentralization, local responsibility and control, and especially nonstatist solutions to economic ills are morally relevant lessons all incorporated into the reform. It is precisely attempts of this sort of thinking, in which moral analysis is combined with orthodox economic theory and practice, that I think represents the best opportunity to advance the cause of justice. I would hope that many others will also develop their own ideas in this way.

Corporate Responsibility

It is spiritually eviscerating that what millions of men and women do fifty or seventy hours of most every week is bracketed off from their understanding of their faith.[5]

A Christian social theology that lacks a theology of the large corporation will have no effective means of inspiring those Christians who do work within large corporations to meet the highest practicable Christian standards.[6]

In and through the modern corporation, many persons today earn their living and find their personal fulfillment. Corporations must and in measure do provide for the well being of human persons, treated equally in their basic dignity, who are social in nature, who have spiritual aspirations and bodily needs, who exercise creativity and freedom, who are limited and sinful.

The corporation is inconceivable except as a cooperative venture in which persons with varied talents freely join together for some creative and common purpose. The corporation will "turn a profit" and survive if its goods or service in some way meets the spiritual or bodily needs of potential buyers. It is through the modern corporation, some small and some very large indeed, that the modern world has witnessed a very new phenomenon: a steadily rising material standard of living. Modern corporations accept the financial costs and risks of bringing goods and services to the marketplace. Corporations finance the research and development costs which must be born to develop a product that meets human needs and which might therefore prove attractive to potential buyers. Corporations are experts in mass production, which is necessary to make good use of scarce resources. Naturally, we could not call inefficiency "good stewardship." Corporations, the engine of capitalism, have historically "delivered the goods," corporations share in God's creativity.

Of course, we must acknowledge the element of human frailty which penetrates all human collectivities, including the modern corporation. Corporations exist as key players within the economic sphere. The ethic that penetrates a corporation is supplied by those persons in authority who determine its corporate culture, which can only reflect the strengths and weaknesses of the larger moral-cultural order. The importance of the churches, civic organizations, and families is clear and is the key to the ethic of the economic sector. But we must also look to the political sector to regulate the corporation. The force of law is required since we know that corporations seeking profit may excessively pollute, injure the rights of those inside and outside the corporation, upset or damage the larger social ethos, and commit other injuries. In other words, the economic sphere is conditioned by the political and moral-cultural spheres. The reverse is also true, highlighting the importance of an entire political, moral, and cultural system which is guided by appropriate moral principles. We are not interested in reforms of the older type, which look to "just" activity on behalf of the central political authority to compensate for unjust activity on behalf of the economic sector (a Rawlsian solution) so that the system as a whole may be called "just." Any reform must actually help make the economic sector itself a contributing participant to good ethics.

So we do not look only to law (politics) but also to the ethics which is set in the moral-cultural sector to guide corporate life. Within the corporation itself we must also find concern for ethical direction. The element of personal commitment in the sense of commitment of the members to one another as persons and commitment of this "community" to the wider common good is essential. Persons find fulfillment in their joint projects not strictly on the basis of self-interest, but out of commitment to other persons within the community and also through the knowledge that the common good is somehow served through joining.

Those who work within corporations must sense that they truly belong; the all-too-common sense of alienation from the workplace must be dealt with. Labor should not be (under) valued as "one economic resource among others" which can be purchased or let go quickly and easily. An attitude of valuing labor and commitment must come to suffuse the modern workplace. Furthermore, not only must the corporation view its workers as valued partners in the enterprise, but it must come to view those unemployed in light of their potential contributions. It must be more eager to bring in the unemployed into the cycle of production and exchange. A Personalist perspective then would look for the following in corporate reform:

1. An appreciation of the social nature of the human person leads us to the realization that solidarity among workers should be advanced and not impeded. Human sociality requires that workers see themselves as sharing a common fate. Although a healthy sense of competition is a good thing, it hardly exhausts the proper mode of relating even among workers who compete within the marketplace.
2. With out integral theological anthropology, the importance of the meeting of human needs cannot be slighted. Corporate efficiency should be enhanced as the condition for the possibility of meeting the needs of those employed. Workers must be enabled to meet their needs and the needs of their families; this is, of course, impossible should the firm fail for lack of ability to compete. Furthermore, the inefficient firm which is led into failure makes no positive contribution to the common good. Finally, inefficiency represents a poor use of scarce resources and hence bad "stewardship."
3. As creative and free human subjects, workers should enjoy participation, as appropriate, in the fundamental decisions which impact them and which govern the direction of the firm.

The full creativity and freedom of human persons cannot be realized in an environment characterized by a lack of participation and by a sense of alienation.

4. Reforms must see the market as an acceptable basis with which to meet human needs. Reforms must be cognizant of the development within Catholic Social Thought on its more positive reassessment of market institutions.

5. Reforms should be contextual and congruent with the present American situation. The reforms must not only attack those ills, including, but not limited to, unemployment and low wages, but must also show awareness of the lessons of past attempts to deal with these same ills. As became clear in chapter 2, the importance of decentralization, local responsibility and control, and especially nonstatist solutions to economic ills are lessons which we have learned by experience since the New Deal and the redistributionist agenda.

The "share economy"[7] refers to a system of worker participation and profit sharing, the idea for which originated in economics with economist Martin Weitzman (MIT). I believe this system contains the seeds for an appropriate Personalist vision for economic life. I offer this chapter to do my part in laying a foundation to displace the worn emphasis on "distributive justice" achieved through the tax transfer arm of the central political authorities.

The Share Economy

The primary argument that Martin Weitzman makes in *The Share Economy* is that through a change in the structure of employee compensation, it would be possible to bring about higher levels of output and employment without inflation over the course of the business cycle than what we frequently experience under the current structure of employee compensation. The recurring macroeconomic problems of unemployment and inflation may be remedied or at least lessened by certain actions taken at the microeconomic level. Recent U.S. economic experience has been one in which the business cycle has brought periods of relative growth in output and employment (such is now the case as I write this book) and also periods of economic stagnation or significant price inflation, or both. According to Weitzman, an economy in which wages depended on profits would be less subject to the cyclical economic contractions. Weitzman summarizes his thesis in this way:

> The thesis of this book is simple. A basic change in employee-compensation arrangements is required to assure that reasonable price stability is compatible with reasonably full employment. So long as we persist in restricting policy options to the usual measures of aggregate fiscal and monetary policy, we will not be able to conquer stagflation. That task is well beyond the range of conventional tools of macroeconomic management.[8]

To conquer stagflation is not to experience temporary relief, but to lessen or eliminate it over the course of the entire business cycle. Lest we become too glib during the peak of a business cycle, we should recall that the severity of recessions, or troughs in the business cycle, tends roughly to be proportionate to the previous peak. Recently, Federal Reserve Chairman Alan Greenspan warned of the return of stagflation—"the U.S. economy was impressive, but faces the opposing dangers of rising inflationary pressures and a possibly severe drag on growth due to Asia's crisis."[9] Shocks to aggregate demand (total spending on goods and services) and the reality of the business cycle come at a very great human cost.

The above is Weitzman's primary thesis. He also makes a second argument in his book although less systematically. The change to a system which bases wages, at least in part, on profits would be very likely to have other effects considered desirable from Weitzman's point of view. Most importantly, under such a system it is likely that in the resource market, labor will come to be valued more, and there will be somewhat less priority given to the product market. Employers will come to care about their workers much like they care about their customers, which is socially desirable from Weitzman's perspective. Effects such as these are central for our purposes.

Strong support for the basic ideas put forth by the "share economy" idea have appeared in the (economic) literature since Weitzman published his book on the subject. Empirical studies have indeed found that profit sharing increases productivity.[10] When groups of employees are covered by such variable pay plans, their employment variability has been found to be lower.[11] It has also been argued forcefully that the potential macrostabilizing effects of profit sharing provide an adequate rationale for public intervention to promote such a system:

> For economists, the main rationales for government intervention in markets are externalities, positive or negative. In either case, the full impact of economic actor's behavior is not captured or felt by those actors. Thus public policies might correct an existing market failure . . . features that improve macro performance—e.g., Weitzman-style employment stabilization benefits not captured by the firm—are candidates for subsidy. Profit sharing plans (and certain associated gain sharing plans) but not ESOPs are likely to have these macro externalities.[12]

Weitzman has made his book accessible to a "wide audience"[13] and so I will gear my discussion here so that it requires roughly the same level of competence in economics.[14] One course each in macro- and microeconomics would be sufficient for at least a basic understanding. The theological ethicist who has never enrolled in the introductory college sequence in economics[15] may miss some details here, but I ask also this reader to bear with me nonetheless. Genuine headway toward a new economic ethic cannot be made without some use of economic concepts, and the substance of the argument presented here is not difficult.

The Present System: Monopolistic Competition

Weitzman believes that the structure of most American markets is best described by the model of "monopolistic competition." It is important to understand what is meant by this. The major market models differ only according to the varying structures of product demand that face the firm.[16] As sole producer, the monopolist faces the entire market demand curve; the monopolist must lower price to sell additional units of a product, or it may sell fewer units and raise price. The firm in a perfectly competitive market has no such market power; it simply must accept the market product price since its output only meets a small portion of the total demand. According to Weitzman, monopolistic competition best describes most American markets. Monopolistically, competitive markets lie in-between monopoly and perfect competition, but closer to competition.

For the monopolist, marginal revenue, the revenue associated with an additional unit of output sold, is less than price (average revenue) because an additional sale requires that the product price be lowered somewhat for all units sold. Therefore, additional sales do not raise total revenue by the full amount of the price. Without government regulation, such companies could restrict output and raise price to increase profits. Utility companies for electricity, gas, and water are classic examples of monopolies.

The firm in perfect competition must accept the going price for its product as determined in the marketplace. This is so because the firm has many rivals producing equivalent products. On the one hand customers could shop elsewhere if higher prices are charged, and on the other hand the firm would never charge less than the market price since it can sell all that it produces at that price. The firm has no market power and no "price policy" over which it has meaningful discretion.

Like the monopolist, the monopolistic competitor does have some market power because it produces a differentiated product for which there are no perfect substitutes. Marginal revenue is therefore slightly less than price. Unlike the monopolist, it has many rivals and the firm therefore has less market power to manipulate price and output for the purpose of profit maximization. The larger the share of the market which the firm occupies (monopoly being the extreme example) and the more differentiated the product, the greater the market power. The monopolistically competitive firm also has many rivals producing close substitute products. But unlike the firm in perfect competition, the monopolistic competitor does indeed have a limited degree of market power and can influence price and output to maximize profits. It need not accept a market price at which it must sell its output. The firm produces a somewhat differentiated product and occupies a significant percentage of the total market share. The firm may sell more by charging less—and would always be willing to sell more at the existing price (if it could). The demand (price) curves and marginal revenue curves facing these firms may be viewed as in figure 5.1. So the monopolistically competitive firm must lower price somewhat to sell more output, and it may raise price if it wishes to sell less.

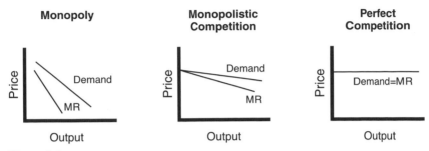

Figure 5.1

If, as Weitzman assumes, the dominant form of market structure in the American economy is best described as monopolistically competitive, then an understanding of how certain fundamental decisions are made in this structure is of great importance. It is also important to understand the product markets because, as we shall see shortly, Weitzman's proposal is that the labor market should be turned into such a market. Weitzman lists three important decisions which these firms make.[17]

(1) How much output to produce;
(2) How much labor to hire;
(3) What price to charge.

These decisions are made according to the following criteria:[18]

(1) Output is selected at the level where marginal revenue equals marginal cost;
(2) As much labor is hired as is needed to produce that output;
(3) Price is set by multiplying marginal cost times the markup coefficient.

Let us review each of these three.

Revenue and cost information are necessary to determine the profit maximizing level of output and, except for perfect competition, for the firm to set price. The profit maximizing rule which applies to firms in all market structures is the famous MC=MR formula. Marginal costs (MC), the costs associated with an additional unit of output, must be equal to marginal revenue (MR), the revenue associated with an additional level of output, if there is to be profit maximization. This is not difficult to understand. If marginal revenue is greater than marginal costs, the firm can increase total profits by producing additional output; if marginal revenue is less than marginal costs, the firm would increase total profits by producing less output. The actual point of operation will be determined by the intersection of marginal cost and marginal revenue as depicted in figure 5.2.

If we have determined the appropriate (profit maximizing) level of output, then we have also decided how many workers to hire. Labor is a variable input which may be hired in greater or lesser amounts to vary production levels.

Price is set by multiplying marginal cost times the markup coefficient. The markup coefficient is the ratio of price to marginal revenue. Weitzman explains price determination this way:

> Since average revenue equals price and since marginal revenue equals marginal cost in a profit-maximizing state, the profit-maximizing ratio of price to marginal cost is also given by the markup coefficient. This means that the firm follows the simple pricing rule of marking up its marginal production cost by a numerical factor (which essentially depends upon the elasticity of demand), hence the term "markup coefficient".[19]

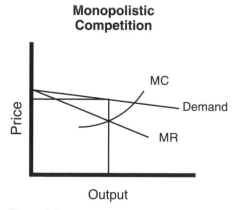

Figure 5.2

Weitzman's perspective makes the setting of price appear somewhat mechanical. It should be noted though that elasticity of demand is not assumed to be constant and the markup coefficient will vary at every point along a demand curve.

Macroeconomic conditions will affect decisions made by our profit-maximizing monopolistically competitive firm. If product demand should decline uniformly at every price and if marginal cost is approximately constant over relevant ranges (which are approximately correct empirical assumptions), then the firm will adjust to the new structure of demand primarily through a change in output and employment with little or no change in price. My own diagrammatic interpretation of this is given in figure 5.3.

Macroeconomics and a Dazzling Policy Digression

Because monopolistic competition is the dominant form of market organization in American capitalism and because monopolistic competition responds to changes in the structure of demand primarily through changes in output and employment, it may be said that the primary effect of the business cycle in American capitalism is to cause large numbers of workers to lose jobs.

In the long run, of course, a decrease in aggregate demand will eventually bring about a lower nominal level of prices and wages. A

RESPONSE TO A CHANGE IN PRODUCT DEMAND

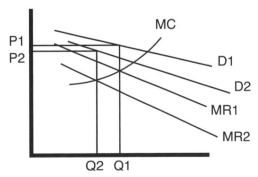

Figure 5.3

return to full employment will then ensue. But the primary short-run adjustment is clear with respect to the real variables of output and employment. Of course, Keynes understood this to be the fundamental problem in a depression. The automatic self-adjusting mechanism within the market system could only work very slowly to bring the economy back up to full employment This is particularly true with respect to the downward rigidity of wages; workers do not easily accept pay cuts which might restore full employment. Keynes's solution then was primarily a call for expansionary fiscal policy (i.e., increased government spending and less taxation).

Consistent with the overall perspective of this book, Weitzman sees Keynes's solution as a digression from the real problem. Thanks to Keynes, discussion among economists about the level of nominal wages had been replaced by discussion about discretion fiscal policy. Today, however, it is necessary to implement structural changes in the manner in which labor is paid if the problems of American capitalism are to be confronted successfully:

> The effect of the Keynesian critique was profound. Pigou himself conceded as much when he wrote, a year after The General Theory: "Until recently no economist doubted that an all-around reduction in the rate of money wages might be expected to increase, and an all-around enhancement to diminish, the volume of employment." Like a great magician, Keynes removed the wage issue from center stage and replaced it by discretionary government policy to manage aggregate demand.
>
> In the long course of history I think this disappearing act must increasingly come to be viewed as something of a dazzling digression from the main route to economic prosperity. Detours are necessary, of course, when the primary road is impassable (and, let us hope, being repaired). But no matter how rough and intractable it may appear at first glance, sooner or later the wage issue must be confronted head on. How labor is paid remains the central issue.[20]

Weitzman's Proposal

Weitzman proposes linking worker compensation, at least in part, to the economic well-being of the firm. This may be done on a profit- or revenue-sharing basis. The worker might receive some base wage which is guaranteed and a share of profits or revenues as well. This "share system" as Weitzman calls it would have important economic properties in a system such as ours. According to Weitzman, firms would adjust to changes in the level of aggregate demand primarily through changes in nominal prices and wages and not in real output and employment.

Let us assume that a given firm converts to the share system and pays workers a base wage plus a specified percentage of profits so that the total compensation to the worker is exactly the same as before under the wage system. Under the wage system in a competitive labor market, the average cost of labor (the wage rate) is equal to the marginal resource cost of labor (the cost of an additional worker). However, in the share system this is no longer true. If more workers are hired, the average level of compensation must decline because the price of the product must decline in order to sell more output and profits are spread out over a larger number of workers. Therefore, the marginal resource cost of labor (MRC) is less than the wage rate. This is analogous to the product market where the demand curve facing the firm is negatively sloped and the marginal revenue curve lies beneath it. I believe that figure 5.4 is an accurate microeconomic representation of Weitzman's proposal.

Marginal revenue product (the addition to total revenue attributable to the hiring of an extra worker) under the share system is greater than the marginal resource cost. This is always an incentive for the firm to expand the hiring of labor from N to N' (above) under the existing labor contract if there are any unemployed workers to be found. Just as the firm in monopolistic competitive would always be willing to sell more at the existing price (if it can), the firm is willing to hire more labor under the existing contract (if it can). Short-run profits are always to be had by finding a willing unemployed worker. Then in the long run we expect the profits to be squeezed out by rising compensation rates as workers bargain for compensation levels that exist at other firms.

Now, let us assume that there are worsening macroeconomic conditions in order to see the short-run reaction of the firm to a moderate decrease in demand for its product. Because the firm (in equilibrium) is in a state of "excess demand for labor"[21] (the firm would like to

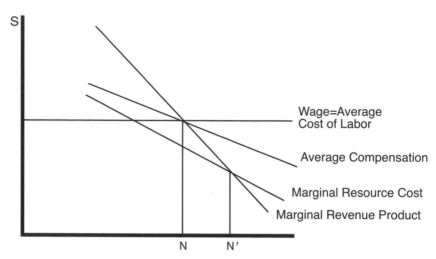

Figure 5.4   The Firm's Supply and Demand for Labor

expand to N' under the existing contract), a "buffer" exists with which to absorb any decrease in product demand. The firm will not force workers from their jobs, although some may seek employment elsewhere if higher compensation can be found (only an enormous decrease in MRP might exhaust the buffer and bring about a lay off). In the face of lower product demand, the tendency will be for the firm to lower price and maintain output and employment. Weitzman provides a numerical example which will allow us to review the micro-economic workings of his proposal.[22]

It is assumed that output is proportional to labor input, and, for purposes of simplification, labor is assumed to be the only input. Initially, General Motors is in equilibrium paying the economywide prevailing wage of $24 per hour including benefits (column c of table 5.1 below) with an employment level of .5 million (column k). Average revenue, or price, for one hour's worth of output, is $36 (column d). Total labor costs are $12 million (column h) and total revenue is $18 million (column g), leaving total profits of $6 million (column i).

Let us now say that GM is hit with a 10-percent decline in product demand. We concluded (above) that the primary effect of a decrease in demand under the wage system is to cause large numbers of

*Table 5.1   Response to a Decline in Product Demand
under Wage and Share Systems*

	a. MRP	b. $(16; \frac{2}{9} \times d)$ Base; Share	c. Total Hourly Pay	d. Average Revenue (per hr. of output)	e. Markup Coef.	f. MRC
Initial:	$24	$16;8	$24	$36	1.5	21.33
Share:	23.20	16;7.73	23.73	35	1.5	21.16
Wage:	24	n.a.	24	63.67	1.5	24

	g. $(d \times k)$ Total Revenue (in millions)	h. $(c \times k)$ Labor Cost (in millions)	i. Profit (in millions)	j. Product Price	k. Employment
Initial:	$18	$12	$6	100%	500,000
Share	17.4	11.865	5.535	$96\frac{2}{3}$ %[23]	500,000
Wage	16.2	10.8	5.4	100%	450,000

workers to lose jobs. Given constant marginal costs and a uniform decline in product demand, the adjustment to the new lower level of demand will primarily entail a drop in output. That is, disequilibrium manifests itself in unemployment and not in changes in wages and prices in a wage system such as ours. The hourly wage remains stable at $24. Because output is proportional to labor, a 10 percent fall in product demand will reduce employment from .5 million to .45 million under the wage system. This reduces total revenue to $16.2 million where labor cost is $10.8 million and profit is $5.4 million.

Under the share system, the short-run adjustment is very different. Let us now assume that the same initial wage rate ($24), which is the prevailing market wage for the skill level of these workers, consists of a base pay of $16 and a share payment. The share percentage is negotiated to be two-ninths of average revenue per employee or $8. We note now that under the share system, GM has equilibriated in a state of "excess demand for labor." This is so because the MRC of labor under the share contract is only $21.33 ($16 + $\frac{2}{9}$ × 24) while the MRP is $24. The short-run, profit-maximizing response to the same decrease in demand is to maintain output and employment levels while lowering product price. Average wage levels fall automatically. This is the profit-maximizing response because marginal revenue product of the extra worker is $23.20 while the marginal cost of the worker is only $21.16. This reduces total revenue to $17.4 million where labor cost is $11.865 million and profit is $5.535 million. Hourly wage is reduced to $23.73.

Let us assume that market wages in this industry continue to be $24. In the long run, if wages at odds with market rates are paid by any firm, we can expect labor negotiations to result in a resetting of the contract with respect to the base wage and/or the profit-sharing parameter. If a disparity still exists, then labor will migrate from lower paying jobs to higher paying ones. That migration by itself would raise compensation for the workers at GM. In the long run, there is no difference between a wage system and a share system; labor will be worked to the point where compensation equals the marginal revenue product. Labor hiring, output, and price will be identical in both cases. There is only a difference in the short run in which worker compensation is affected by the hiring of additional workers. The share system has not altogether eliminated repercussions to the shock, but disequilibrium has taken a different, less painful, form.

A comparison between the two cases reveals that the parties have fared better under the share system in this example. After the shock to product demand, labor as a whole receives $1.065 million more under a share contract than under a wage contract. Profits are also $.135 million more under the share contract. Of course, employment remained constant under the share contract while falling 10 percent under the wage contract. Workers overall will be grateful for employment stability. Even though all seem to be winners if the firm converts to a share contract, we can spot potential losers. Even though labor benefits as a class, those workers who are more skilled and probably better tenured would most likely have fared better under a wage contract. They would have been the last to receive the boot in the case of a shock to demand. They would likely have retained their jobs at hourly wages which remained rigid at $24 compared to the share contract in which wages would fall.

On the basis of the protection and promotion of the common good, the central political authority ought to intervene against narrow self-interest (and lack of class consciousness) on the part of those who are lucratively employed. At this point it is important to recall the Personalist notion of social justice developed in the previous chapter. While I did not wish unnecessarily to exaggerate my differences with Novak (I do agree with the core insight that social justice ought not be seen as a *static principle* of social organization, and I also agree quite strongly that the achievement of the common good will involve the expansion of civil society and the contraction of centralized political authority.), I did conclude that Novak's reluctance to offer a more substantive vision of the common good is very problematic because the processes and outcomes of collective behavior will lack a well-grounded normative yardstick. Structural criticism and reform are more difficult to make both theoretically and practically. I do not agree that the common good will necessarily be achieved through the free choices and contrary purposes of individuals. Free persons must step forward and assume collective responsibility for the final shape of the structures which they bring into being. This will involve observation, understanding, criticism, and *visionary* action guiding the system as a whole. One does not necessarily speak of implementing a "draconian scheme"[24] when one says that a (Personalist) vision can be systematically advanced using the powers of the state to enable civil society and nonviolently to *guide* movement toward (not implementation of) this vision. It seems unwise to ignore the repeated assertions within Catholic Social Thought about the need for a central authority repeated assertions within Catholic Social Thought about the need for a central authority that does enable, guide, and course correct as necessary.

One is tempted to think that the key factor in Weitzman's proposal is what might be seen as a return to the assumption of the more ideal market situation of flexible wages and prices of the classical economists which guarantees full employment. This, however, is not the case. It is not the automatic pay cut per se that serves to maintain short-run output and employment in the case of a shock to demand. The fact that the firm can be said to stabilize in a state of "excess demand for labor" is the important factor according to Weitzman:

Note that it is not the automatic pay cut per se which drives the whole example. If pay were lowered by 1.1 percent on a straight wage contract, that would only save 3.3 percent of GM jobs (a 1.1 percent wage or price change times a demand elasticity of 3), a far cry from the 10 percent actually saved. . . .

Thus the share system does not eliminate unemployment by in effect lowering wages to the point where equilibrium is automatically maintained. The driving force behind full employment in a share system is not the actual lowering of pay during a recessionary shock, but rather the potential lowering that would occur if more workers could be hired. (This is what drives a wedge between marginal and average costs of labor.)[25]

Macroeconomic Implications

We saw that under the wage system the primary effect of the business cycle in American capitalism is to cause large numbers of workers to lose jobs, while the remaining workers received the same compensation as before the drop in demand. Under the share system the primary effect of the business cycle would be to cause a decrease in average compensation and product prices but without the painful reduction in employment. Under the share system firms would adjust to a drop in demand with falling prices and stable employment. This also reduces the second-round drop in aggregate demand which would occur through lay offs with a multiplier effect. If the share system works as advertised, then the system will produce a permanent labor shortage in which firms have a profit-maximizing motive to behave as "vacuum cleaners," sucking up unemployed workers even in downturns of the business cycle. Firms would always be on the prowl, looking for unemployed workers. A perceived labor shortage would be expected to persist in a mild recession and would surely outperform a wage system in this and other cases.

There is, however, another likely benefit from the share system which concerns the full employment level but does not pertain directly to the business cycle. It is very likely that the "natural rate of unemployment"[26] would be reduced. That is, *stable prices* might be consistent with a lower level of unemployment. Weitzman argues that there are three ways in which a share system could help to reduce the natural rate of unemployment.[27]

According to one theory, the increase in the natural rate can in part be attributed to those who have experienced situations of long-term unemployment and now face special obstacles in returning to the workforce. These persons may have experienced a deterioration of their skills and work ethic, and/or society has forgotten about their plight and does not assist them. A share system would help such persons. A share system would make the initial period of unemployment less likely, and the built-in "vacuum cleaner" effect would be more likely to offer such persons employment.

Another theory about the rise in the natural rate argues that organized labor has gained excessive bargaining power. Under the share system, management would retain control of employment decisions and would be free to hire more labor at any time. Of course, labor that is employed has some incentive to oppose the hiring of additional personnel because it would dilute the size of the individual share payment. If bargaining between management and labor over employment is not allowed (being restricted to issues of wages and share percentages), then the share system would produce a lower natural rate.

Third, a share system would help to reduce the frictional and structural unemployment caused by the permanent presence of microeconomic changes in a market economy. Industries that begin to experience decreased demand will not tend to terminate workers, however, workers in such industries will see the share component of their compensation reduced. Just as in a wage system, over time labor will have an incentive to move from the less profitable to the more profitable industries. The difference is that the worker has more options in the short run because she does not immediately lose employment in a share system.

With such great potential in combating cyclical and structural unemployment, one might ask why market economies have not abandoned the current wage system and established a share system. Weitzman's answer is that the cyclical macroeconomic aspect of the wage system appears as an externality to private business. This penalty attached to a wage system will be endured by the economy as a whole, and the market system does not incorporate such externalities into the planning and decision making that occurs in the market. This is, therefore, sufficient grounds for the national government to encourage the growth of share systems of labor compensation. Weitzman suggests that the share portion of wages might be taxed differently (at a lower rate) which would encourage firms in a relatively voluntary and noncoercive way to move toward a share system.

Soft-Boiled Reasons for a Share Economy

Alienation of workers, the power of capital over labor, and the reserve army of the unemployed are specific consequences of the wage mode, not universal characteristics of the capitalist system. Sooner or later it will be realized that a share version of capitalism greatly outperforms a wage version, and something will be done about it.[28]

I mentioned earlier that Weitzman makes a second major argument in his book. Under a share system, it is likely that significant changes in human relations would occur. This argument is very important for our purposes. Weitzman borrows language from Marx when he speaks of the alienation of workers, the power of capital over labor, and the reserve army of the unemployed, but he has given the terms a less shrill and more relevant interpretation, I believe. Let us consider Weitzman's reasoning.

Weitzman argues that there are three reasons why employee compensation ought to be linked to performance. Analogous to eggs, there are soft-boiled, medium-boiled, and hard-boiled reasons for preferring a share system:

A "soft-boiled" reason is that gain sharing (contingent compensation schemes) can boost employee morale, increase worker participation, improve labor-management relations, foster a sense of partnership, raise productivity, and so forth. . . . Note that the benefits in the soft-boiled version are strictly private, so there is no really legitimate case for social policy. . . .

A "medium-boiled" argument holds that gain sharing is good simply because greater aggregate wage flexibility is desirable per se. When wages are automatically made more sensitive to economic conditions, so goes the argument, that cannot help improving macroeconomic performance. . . .

A share system has the "hard-boiled" property of excess demand for labor, which turns it into a tenacious natural enemy of stagnation and inflation.[29]

The hard- and medium-boiled reasons for preferring a share system were discussed above and they relate primarily to considerations of efficiency. With little loss of meaning, one might read ethical reasons excluding efficiency instead of soft-boiled reasons. These ethical reasons especially concern us here, and we want to examine what Weitzman anticipates would be the likely result of a share system in this respect. The literature to this point has almost exclusively analyzed the hard-boiled aspects of the proposed share system.

Valuing Labor

Weitzman views monopolistic competition as a situation of "excess supply of goods" and an "excess supply of labor." Because price exceeds marginal cost (unlike pure competition), the firm in monopolistic competition would always be willing to sell more at the existing price (excess supply of goods), which leads firms to advertise greatly and leads salesperson in a typical business to treat prospective buyers very well. The experience of a customer in a new car dealership illustrates this well. A very congenial salesperson will greet the customer with the most helpful of attitudes. Customers find that salespersons show a genuine interest in tailoring an automotive package to suit their needs and desires. Delivery, complex financing, and other aspects of the purchase are worked out for maximal convenience to the customer in this buyer's paradise. However, if we should pass into the repair/service shop, we find that the business treats its labor very differently. We are likely to find a poor, dirty, environment. There is no extraordinary effort to please the workers. Decision making is centralized in management. There is little concern about organizing work schedules and wage payment options for maximal convenience to the worker. We have "two different worlds of human relations."[30] One could say that there is, properly understood, a certain fetishism of commodities and exploitation of labor.

The incentive to the firm under a share system would be to treat labor very differently. The firm under a share contract is always willing to hire more labor under the existing contract. This excess demand for labor would provide a strong incentive for the firm to attract workers much like it does buyers of its products. There would be as much emphasis in treating labor well as in selling output. The two different worlds of human relations might begin to converge (see figure 5.5):[31]

Under the share system, the firm finds that it is in its (profit maximizing) interest to find and retain personnel. Hired personnel become valued much like customers are valued by monopolistically competitive firms. Alienation of workers is reduced. Empirical studies do cite a key predictor of the incidence of profit sharing: the managerial philosophy of the firm.[32] Managers trained in an *industrial humanistic management school* of thought are most receptive to profit sharing.[33]

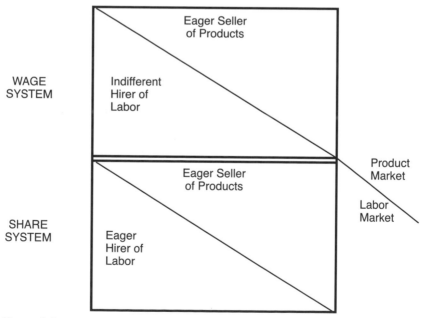

Figure 5.5

Discrimination

Women and minorities continue to experience higher rates of unemployment than the population as a whole. Weitzman believes that a share system would likely reduce race and sex discrimination in a way that orders from the central government and the courts have been unable to effect:

> It (i.e., excess demand for labor) gives dignity to the working man and woman, the sense of being significant, useful members of society. . . . The worker's greatest protection is his power to get a job elsewhere—that threat can do more to improve working conditions than legislation, standards, or collective militancy.[34]

During the labor shortage of the Second World War, the unemployment rate reached its lowest point of the century. Government and industry worked as vacuum cleaners searching for pockets of unemployment. Women and minorities were accepted and wanted in the workforce. All legislation since then has been unable to do for women and minorities what the labor shortage of the 1940s did. The political sector has failed to bring an end to various sorts of discrimination.

Under a share system, we are likely to witness the end of what might loosely be called "the reserve army of the unemployed." As during the Second World War, employers would no longer have the luxury of selecting employees according to discriminatory criteria because of the high demand and the diminished pool of applicants.

Class Conflict

Struggles on the part of different groups for a larger share of the economic pie are a continuing reality in market economies. The struggle may be a reality, but in a wage system the struggle between capital and labor remains somewhat hidden. Wage rates seem to reflect (impersonal) market forces, and what some people have called exploitation or expropriation by capital of what rightfully belongs to labor is a difficult reality to identify and quantify in a wage system.

Such struggles on the part of different groups for a larger share of the economic pie would continue to be a reality in market economies under a share system. At the same time, it has been pointed out by James Tobin that such struggles would become more explicit under a share system:

> In some countries (maybe not in our own, but very likely in Britain) inflation is symptomatic of a fundamental disharmony about the division of the national pie, even of a failure to agree on a process by which its distribution is to be determined. That basic disharmony is not resolved either by reducing the size of the pie or by increasing it. You get inflation as a result, but inflation is not necessarily corrected very soon or very fundamentally by depression, even by large reductions in employment and output. So basic a disharmony would show up clearly in Weitzman's economy in fights about s.[35] Fights that are disguised in a wage system could be naked struggles in the Weitzman system in a country like Britain. Maybe that is good because it means that the parties have to face the problem of resolving these conflicts outright.[36]

Because it makes explicit an ongoing argument and can only serve to improve the quality of the discussion, I count this characteristic of a share economy as a good and not an evil.

New Responsibility for Unions

When labor works simply for a fixed wage, it tends to be seen as simply one among other inputs that enters into the production process and is compensated accordingly. Labor bears less responsibility and has little immediate interest in the final outcome at the end of the fiscal year. Under a share system, it is necessary for the employer to open the books and discuss relevant information about profits. Otherwise, it would be impossible for labor to know if the magnitude of the share payments is correct. Continuing along this line, Daniel Mitchell has pointed out that this process would likely begin to involve labor in the decision-making process in a more formal way:

> It is only a step from access to information to critiquing what that information reveals. If company profits were to drop, it is likely that the union would want to know the reason for the decline, not merely

that it had occurred. At the company level, profitability will responds to more than the economy-wide business cycle; it will also
reflect managerial decisions. A share system inevitably opens up
questions of shared decision making as well as shared financial
outcomes.[37]

These things are important to note since labor has at times been
unsure of the share system. However, we should not conclude that
this new role for labor would increase prices and unemployment. The
share system does not result only in the expansion of union power
since unions must largely agree to give up prohibitions, where they
exist, against the hiring of new workers. Furthermore, the expansion
of union power need not be associated with ever rising prices since
labor agrees to tie its own compensation (the largest single cost for
the typical firm) to firm profitability.

Capital Markets

Empirical evidence supports the idea that improvements in profit
margins and stock prices appear to increase the chance of profit-sharing adoption by a given company.[38] It is believed that profit-sharing
plans are a prudent means to increase labor compensation in periods
of relative company prosperity without obliging the company to a
fixed increase into the indefinite future. This protects the company in
case of profit downturn when meeting such stiff obligations which
would not correspond to its present condition and might potentially
be financially ruinous. Relatively high stock prices and economic
expansion (which are the case at the time of this writing) represent an
opportunity for the adoption of a share system.

Not at all surprisingly, *after* adoption the empirical evidence is that
profit sharing tends to be associated on average with further increase
in productivity.[39] This too is a powerful argument in favor of the
adoption of profit sharing in the minds of stockholders. There is,
however, variability among firms with respect to any such productivity gains. Firms which do not emphasize an environment of trust,
commitment, and communication are less likely to realize such productivity gains. The benefits inherent in profit sharing are, therefore,
underexploited. For this reason, it is believed that enlightened man-

agement styles should precede or at least accompany the adoption of a profit-sharing method for compensation.

Additionally, Weitzman may have understated some of the benefits accrued to the firm from profit sharing which will likely enhance the value of its stock. For Weitzman, the main reasons for government intervention in markets are externalities in which the impact of economic actors' behavior is not captured or felt by those actors. Thus, public policies might correct such spillover costs or *benefits* to optimize market performance from the standpoint of the common good (in our case, to encourage Weitzman-style profit-sharing programs to gain the macroemployment stabilization benefits). However, it has been argued[40] that precisely this reduction in variation of company output and employment is also a benefit to the firm and its shareholders. Reduction in these variations can help firms retain employee skills in which the firm has vested interest and increase employee loyalty. Reductions in these variations are attractive to stockholders since higher risk by itself is a disincentive to the holding of shares.

So although I believe the strongest arguments favoring the share system relate to the protection and promotion of the common good, most individuals and most groups that we designate more broadly as "capital and labor" also stand to benefit.

Soft-Boiled Reasons against a Share Economy

Having looked at the soft-boiled (ethical) reasons for a share economy, we must also discuss possible ethics-related issues against a share economy. There are isolated groups that may oppose reforms that promote the common good but injure certain minoritarian groups.

Senior Workers

As already mentioned by Weitzman, the potential losers in a share system might be those workers who are more skilled and probably better tenured. This is particularly true if we assume a union setting that has guaranteed preferential treatment to senior employees. These employees are least likely to lose their jobs in the case of a shock to demand. In a wage system they would likely retain their jobs with no change in hourly wages compared to the share contract in which wages would fall. So we have identified at least one group that might oppose a share system based on self-interest.

This group might seek to oppose a share system entirely, or the group could attempt to build in protection for itself so that it fares at least as well in a share system when compared to the wage system. Regrettably, the impact of any significant social policy involves various double effects and trade offs. I recommend that prudential compromises be reached as a share economy is encouraged and that some protection be given to these disproportionately powerful groups in the short run. Viewed from the perspective of labor as a whole, and certainly from the perspective of the overall common good, opposition to the share economy for these reasons could only be considered the most narrow form of self-interest and denial of any reasonable interpretation of "class consciousness."

The Power of Unions

It is basic to the operation of a share economy that the employer be able to hire additional labor at any time. It is also clear that senior workers may have reason to oppose the hiring of additional personnel because this will reduce the size of the share payment of labor compensation to individual workers. If labor is organized, it might seek to obtain guarantees against hiring of the unemployed. However, this must be forbidden in a share economy. There is then a sense in which labor is being restricted here and denied an issue over which it may bargain. This presents us with an ethical dilemma; Weitzman gives us his ideas:

> The bargaining power of unions is not a natural right. As a matter of fact, throughout labor history in Great Britain and the United States until well into the present century, common-law doctrine held labor unions to be an illegal "conspiracy in restraint of trade." The right of labor to bargain collectively was granted by the state, presumably to improve the welfare of the average working man and woman, only relatively recently as such things go, after years of hard-fought struggle by legions of courageous, downtrodden, underprivileged people seeking work with dignity. . . . The share system is

a better game than the wage system, but played with strict rules; and one of them is that new workers are welcome to join a share firm.

It is unclear just what exactly Weitzman considers to be the appropriate criteria for a natural right, but he defends himself by appealing to the larger purpose of unionization and collective bargaining. The end of unionization and collective bargaining is to ensure the dignity of labor, and bargaining about employment would only appear as a means that is expendable in the new context of a share system. This perspective is quite consistent with that found within Catholic Social Thought which has long maintained the right to labor organization as grounded in the deeper principles of protection of the common good and the universal right of all persons to access to the goods of creation.

Unequal and Variable Income

Many unions and other elements within labor have fought and continue to fight hard for "equal pay for equal work" on the basis of fairness. Daniel Mitchell[41] has pointed out that this goal would have to be forsworn in a share economy. If labor is to have some portion of its total compensation linked to profits (or revenue) then compensation will vary among workers in different firms just as profits (or revenue) varies among different firms. In a share system labor takes on a more mature role and has a stake in the well-being of the business.

At the same time, Mitchell points out that there are senses in which this goal of "equal pay for equal work" might be maintained if it is interpreted loosely. For example, the achievement of equal pay formulas might be interpreted as fulfilling the demand of "equal pay for equal work."

Another corollary to the practice in a share economy of linking labor compensation to the performance of the firm is that compensation to individual workers will be less stable than it would under a wage system. The higher the percentage of total compensation that is given in the form of a share payment, the larger this variability and the lower the wage floor. Although (as discussed) the macroeconomic effects of the share system might protect labor as a group in a way that is superior to a wage system, a share system could still result in very low wages, indeed, being paid at selected firms which are performing badly. Some role for the redistributive state remains, then, in order to insure against catastrophically low income during periods of a partial or a complete loss of regular income.

Prospects for a Share Economy

A share economy has strong potential to gain the public support necessary to institutionalize and maintain it. The political left would likely view this as a positive development for labor in general. The share system gives increased responsibility to labor, reduces unemployment, and has the other favorable effects mentioned above. At the same time, the political right might well view this system as a return to the classical assumption of freely flexible wages and prices which guarantees full employment in a market economy and a reduction in direct government interference in the private sector. Full employment is also likely to generate more than sufficient funds to compensate for the loss in tax revenue to the federal government attributable to preferential treatment given to share income. The economic gains of full employment are quite robust. Because of this argument, Weitzman has referred to himself as a supply sider par excellence:

> This is supply-side economics par excellence. But I would hope that the reader can see that behind it stands a coherent theory and a genuine logic based upon the reemployment of idle resources. The same cannot be said for the cocktail-napkin version proposed by Arthur Laffer and his colleagues.[42]

Initial popular reaction to the share economy has been favorable. Indeed, given the moral and economic advantages of such a system, the next step is simply to make informed appeals to those audiences which will be receptive out of concern for their own gain as well as for national economic prosperity, greater macroeconomic stability, lower cyclical unemployment, a favorable moral transformation of the workplace, and out of a genuine concern for human dignity. Although minoritarian groups with disproportionate power (illustrated for example in the scenario of senior workers objecting to the hiring of new workers) might oppose the share economy out of self-interested politics, the share system almost certainly represents gains materially and morally for the overwhelming numbers of economic participants.

The share economy is a powerful concrete example of a Personalist economic reform agenda. It shows an appreciation of the social nature of the human person and advances solidarity among workers as they share a common fate. It promises to help meet human bodily and material needs since it promises greater micro- and macroeconomic efficiency. As creative and free human subjects, workers experience greater participation in profit sharing and decision making; alienation is thereby reduced. The share economy successfully moves past and around the older Keynesian agenda. Furthermore, the importance of decentralization, local responsibility and control, and especially non-statist (but also nonlibertarian) solutions to economic ills are morally relevant lessons incorporated into the reform.

Conclusion

At the start of this work, I offered the opinion that there is today a remarkable consensus among social ethicists in matters of political economy which has such hegemony that it may well undermine the creativity and relevance of Christian social ethics in addressing contemporary social problems. The primary emphasis of the ethicists under consideration since the time of John Ryan has been to encourage the growth of the welfare state, and it is unusual when a departure from this trajectory of things is given serious or extended consideration. This has resulted in what I believe to be defective theory and detachment from economic evidence and experience. It will appear to many as particularly regrettable since Christianity (and certainly Catholicism) is a sacramental religion which affirms material existence. Moral theory should be realist; it should be informed by as well as speak to actual situations. At the same time, decisions about practical issues should be guided by ethical theory and principles. So although the *substantive* positions taken here are (at present) different and minoritarian within the profession, I believe that the most interesting and primary contribution of this work has been the *method* of integration of moral theory with economic and empirical research.

I argued against the three ideas that market systems are a poor basis on which to meet human needs; that the essential economic problem in a market system is the exploitation of labor by capital; and that justice requires the state to expand its role in economic life. A Christian Personalist moral theory was then developed which would effectively address the situation of American individualism—a moral theory that was capable of incorporating certain liberal insights about the human person while offering constructive criticism of that same liberal perspective. There was an emphasis on community and subsidiarity which not only reflects economic and empirical research, but also the theological commitment that human flourishing happens both *in action* and *in community* with others.

The share economy is illustrative of a solution that takes into account the data of economics as well as moral theory. I have not argued that this vision is the only vision which can claim support from Catholic Social Thought, since there is a very legitimate pluralism around such matters. It is, however, a compelling nonstatist solution which recognizes that the powerful and influential economic sector itself must exhibit just behavior (i.e., we do not rely primarily and first on remediation and redistributionism by the political sector to achieve justice). The powers of the state can be harnessed to *guide* movement toward (not implement) a more humane vision for economic life. Although there will always be a role for the state in the pursuit of justice, the nature and extent of that role must be scrutinized from the standpoints of theory and experience. To sum up, this gives the share economy three categories of advantages: it is a reform agenda consistent with our Christian Personalist theory; it successfully moves past the older Keynesian agenda and "Ryanism"; and the reform reflects the importance of decentralization, local responsibility, and control.

I do mean the solution to be illustrative and not exhaustive, and I hope that it will compete with solutions which others may put forth. At the same time, I am quite convinced that any serious solution will have to demonstrate at least the above three strengths. It seems difficult to imagine a morally acceptable and economically feasible solution which does not contain those characteristics; and I believe that we should look only for reform agendas that are both morally acceptable and economically feasible as we attempt to speak prophetically about the present economic situation.

Notes

1. David Hollenbach, "Unemployment and Jobs: A Theological and Ethical Perspective," in John Houck and Oliver Williams, eds., *Catholic Social Teaching and the United States Economy: Working Papers for a Bishops' Pastoral* (Washington, D.C.: University Press of American, 1984), p.123.

2. John Finnis, *Natural Law and Natural Rights* (Oxford: Clarendon Press, 1980) p.31.

   > For the real problem of morality, and of the point or meaning of human existence, is not in discerning the basic aspects of human well-being, but in integrating those various aspects into the intelligent and reasonable commitments, projects, and actions that go to make up one or other of the many admirable forms of human life.

3. Kate Wendleton is author of a series of career development books: *Targeting the Job You Want* (1997), *Job-Search Secrets* (1997), and *Building a Great Resume* (1997), (Five O'Clock Books, New York).

4. John XXIII, *Mater et Magistra,* par. 65.

5. Richard John Neuhaus, *Doing Well and Doing Good: The Challenge to the Christian Capitalist* (New York: Doubleday, 1992), p.63.

6. Michael Novak, *Toward a Theology of the Corporation* (Washington and London: American Enterprise Institute for Public Policy Research, 1981), p.54

7. Martin Weitzman, *The Share Economy: Conquering Stagflation* (Cambridge, Massachusetts: Harvard University Press, 1984).

8. Weitzman, *The Share Economy,* p.2.

9. Reported by Knut Engelmann (Washington, July 21), Reuters 211542 GMT Jul 1998. Additionally, Greenspan stated: "Conditions in Asia are of particular concern, the economic and financial troubles in Asian economies are now demonstrably restraining demands for U.S. goods and services, and those troubles could intensify and spread further".

10. Seongsu Kim, "Does Profit Sharing Increase Firms' Profits"? *Journal of Labor Research,* vol.19, no.10, spring 1998.

11. Barry Gerhart and Charles O. Trevor, "Employment Variability under Different Managerial Compensation Systems," *Academy of Management Journal,* vol.39, no. 6, December 1996.

12. Daniel Mitchell, "Profit Sharing and Employee Ownership: Policy Implications," *Contemporary Economic Policy,* vol.13, no.2, April 1995, p.2–8.

13. Weitzman, *The Share Economy,* p.v.

14. Because he believes that the message of his book is quite important, Weitzman claims to have written his book in such a way that it is accessible to a wide and interdisciplinary audience. The text requires a mastering of economics only at an elementary level.
15. This will typically include one course in microeconomics and one course in macroeconomics.
16. For the most part, markets are not assumed to differ with respect to the costs of production.
17. Weitzman, *The Share Economy,* p.10
18. Weitzman, *The Share Economy,* p.17.
19. Weitzman, *The Share Economy,* p.18.
20. Weitzman, *The Share Economy,* p.54.
21. It may seem awkward to the reader, as it did to me, to say that a firm equilibrates in a state of excess demand. This is only meant as a heuristic device to say that the marginal cost of labor is less than the average cost. See the criticism of William Nordhaus and the reply of Weitzman in: William Nordhaus and Andrew John, editors, "The Share Economy: A Symposium," *Journal of Comparative Economics,* vol. 10, no. 4, December 1986 pp.414–73.
22. Weitzman, *The Share Economy,* pp.100–6.
23. According to Weitzman, the ratio of P/MR must equal the ratio of elasticity ÷ elasticity − 1. So if the markup coefficient is 1.5, then elasticity is three. If elasticity is three, then a 10 percent decline in quantity is offset only by a $3\frac{1}{3}$ percent decrease in price.
24. Michael Novak, *The Catholic Ethic and the Spirit of Capitalism* (New York: Free Press, 1993) p.85.
25. Weitzman, *The Share Economy,* p.105.
26. Alternative terminology for those who object to "natural rate" exists with the concept of the "nonaccelerating-inflation rate of unemployment" (or NAIRU) determined with a Walrasian equilibrium. His name was Walras, and the equilibrium arguement was named after him.
27. Martin L. Weitzman, "The Share Economy: A Reply," *Journal of Comparative Economics,* vol. 10, no.4, December 1986, pp.469–73.
28. Weitzman, *The Share Economy,* p.122.
29. Weitzman, *The Share Economy,* pp.142–4.
30. Weitzman, *The Share Economy,* p.8.
31. Diagram, in part, from Weitzman, *The Share Economy,* p.94.
32. Richard J. Long, "Motives for Profit Sharing: A Study of Canadian Chief Executive Officers," *Industrial Relations,* vol.52, no.4, fall 1997 (Quebec), pp.712–33.
33. Long summarizes the three major schools of thought:

Miles (1975) has argued that three main schools of managerial thought can be identified—the classical school, the human relations school, and the human resources school (referred to in this paper as the "industrial humanism" school to avoid confusion). The classical manager assumes that people are motivated only by economic self-interest, and will do as little as possible while still maximizing their economic gain. These managers will tend to practice a traditional, tightly controlled approach to management, with individual jobs fragmented into tiny pieces in order to allow easy supervision and replacement of employees. (p.717)

The human relations manager also assumes that work is inherently distasteful, but they believe that employees can best be induced to work by the social rewards that the organization can provide. They will still practice a control-oriented approach to management, with fragmented jobs, but control will be exercised through development of positive group work norms, which will flow from an employee-oriented, paternalistic approach practised by management. Finally, the industrial humanism manager assumes that employees can be self-motivated if their work is challenging and interesting, if they are given sufficient autonomy and organizational support to perform it as they see fit, and if employee goals are integrated with those of the organization. Lawler (1992) terms this third approach the "high involvement" approach to management.

34. Weitzman, *The Share Economy,* p.122.
35. "s" here refers to the percent of profits which goes to labor under a share agreement.
36. James Tobin, "Inflation and Unemployment in the Share Economy," *Journal of Comparative Economics,* vol.10, no.4, December 1986, p.463.
37. Daniel J.B. Mitchell, "The Share Economy and Industrial Relations," *Industrial Relations,* vol.26, no.1, winter 1987, p.14.
38. Douglas L. Kruse, *Profit Sharing, Does It Make a Difference?* (Kalamazoo, Michigan: W.E. Upjohn Institute for Employment Research, 1993), p.148.
39. Kruse, *Profit Sharing, Does It Make a Difference?* p.162.
40. Kruse, *Profit Sharing, Does It Make a Difference?* p.164.
41. Mitchell, *"The Share Economy and Industrial Relations"* p.8.
42. Weitzman, *The Share Economy,* p.132. See also the calculations contained in his footnote number two for chapter 9, p.153–4.

Index